A Chequer-Board
Of
Nights

by

Bill McCrea

First Published 2003

Copyright ©Bill McCrea

ISBN 1900604140

Printed and bound in the United Kingdom

Published by Compaid Graphics
T'otherside, Drumacre Lane East,
Longton, Preston. PR4 4SD.
www.compaidgraphics.co.uk

Cover painting 'Incident Over Hannover'
By Eric Day

Dedication

This book is dedicated to the 55,000 men of Bomber Command who gave their lives so that those who came after had the freedom to question the ethics of their actions.

Contents

List of Photographs

Acknowledgements

First of all, I must acknowledge the encouragement given to me by my wife, Gwyneth, my son John, and my daughter Sheelagh, when I told them I was thinking of setting down on paper the story of my operational tour with Bomber Command in 1943. The story has taken time to write and without their support it would never have been completed. I would like to thank my mid-upper gunner, Chris Allen, and my wireless operator, Joe Coxall, for their contributions. I lost touch with Chris for 43 years and with Joe for 58. It was a delight to meet up with both again; friendships forged among members of a bomber crew last forever. My thanks are also due to Air Commodore Henry Probert, MBE, who read my initial efforts, saw some promise, and told me to carry on. My thanks, too, to the Air Historical Branch of the Ministry of Defence, for confirming some facts that I wished to use in the book. But I am most indebted to Marshal of the Royal Air Force Sir Michael Beetham, GCB, CBE, DFC, AFC, FRAeS, who agreed to read my manuscript and then sent me four pages of helpful observations and suggestions. Sir Michael was not only a distinguished Chief of the Air Staff but also, in his capacity as President of the Bomber Command Association, a worthy successor to 'Butch' Harris as the defender of the men who fought in the bomber war. He had so much success in both these roles that it is easy to overlook his contribution as a Lancaster pilot during Bomber Command's darkest months through the winter of 1943/44. No one is better qualified to comment on what I have written than Sir Michael and I am most grateful for the help and encouragement that he has given me. Finally, if there is any profit from the sale of this book, the greater part will be shared between the Bomber Command Association, which has done so much to counter the post-war vilification of the bomber aircrews and their Commander, and the 57 and 630 Squadrons' Association, whose annual reunions and newsletters have become the focus for the diminishing band of survivors, as well as for the many relatives of those who took off and did not return.

'Tis all a Chequer-Board of Nights and Days
Where Destiny with Men for Pieces plays:
Hither and thither moves, and mates, and slays,
And one by one back in the closet lays.

Rubaiyat of Omar Khayyam

Introduction

It was March 1951. I had received a letter from Hogg Robinson advising me that my car would be arriving at Hamburg Docks on the following Tuesday and asking me to make arrangements for its collection. I had been in Germany for just two weeks, filling a staff post at the Headquarters of the British Air Forces of Occupation. I was not sure I wanted to go to Hamburg. I had never been there before, at least not on the ground, but I had taken part in all four of the Bomber Command raids in the summer of 1943, when I had watched from twenty thousand feet as the city burned below. On the other hand, I needed my Rover Sports. Before leaving England, I had spent a lot of money on a complete engine overhaul and I was looking forward to testing the results on the German autobahns. I took the train to Hamburg and booked in at the 'Four Seasons' Officers' Club which had survived the raids. It had been a club for German officers during the war and now served the same purpose for the Allied Forces. On the following morning, I called up the Forces Taxi Service and was soon taking delivery of my car. I carefully left the dock area, having first fastened a prepared notice to the dashboard reminding me to 'Drive on the Right'.

I spent the next hour driving around Hamburg. The roads had been cleared and repaired, but in between, as far as the eye could see, there was little but heaps of rubble. Here and there, a building was still standing, some were occupied, but they stood out starkly amid the desolation. My drive among the ruins was a sobering experience; I had been responsible in part for this destruction. Stories were filtering through about the effects of the firestorm following the second raid and some officers on the Intelligence Staff had seen German newsreels that left nothing to the imagination. Of course, it had been horrible, but I felt that the Germans were largely to blame. After all, they had started it - on Rotterdam, on Coventry, on London - and when the time came for retribution they made no attempt to evacuate their women and children, hoping perhaps that their continued presence in the towns and cities might be a human shield against attack.

As I drove away from the city, I wondered if Germany would ever again take its place among the nations of Europe. Even after almost six years, the signs of defeat were everywhere. There was a constant movement of people from east to west; many of these were ex-soldiers who had either escaped from the Russian prison camps or perhaps had managed to find a way out of the Russian Zone. I took pity on a one-legged man, who was making slow progress on makeshift crutches, and stopped to offer him a lift. He was reluctant to accept; that an 'offizier' wished to help was beyond belief. We had difficulty in communicating but I gathered he had spent several years with the Russians and they had not treated him well. As I reached the autobahn and dropped him off, I gave him the packed lunch that the 'Four Seasons' had prepared for me that morning. His reaction suggested that he had not eaten for days.

My tour around Hamburg was not my first look at Germany in defeat. Shortly after the end of the war, I had flown a Wellington, with a skeleton crew and as many ground staff aboard as we could manage, on a 'Cook's Tour' of the battle areas. We flew over Holland, where it seemed as if half the country was under water, up the Rhine to Wesel, where Montgomery and his men had crossed the river after the town had been completely obliterated by aerial bombardment. From there to Essen, Dusseldorf and Cologne, towns that used to be approached with apprehension - and even fear - by bomber aircrews, but now lay in ruined impotence below. Then on to Coblenz, before turning around to fly back down the Rhine and view with some amazement the tens of thousands of prisoners herded into enclosures along the eastern bank of the river. This had been Germany in the immediate aftermath of defeat and that defeat had been so complete that the regeneration of the nation had been a slow and painful process. Six years later, the members of the occupying forces were still the victors. They were forbidden to fraternise with the German population, who were still the defeated.

The situation was vastly different in the summer of 1941 ....

Prologue

I never had the remotest intention of joining the British Armed Forces. After all, I lived in neutral Ireland and felt no compulsion to do so. Like millions of others I was fascinated by the Battle of Britain and revelled in the heroic deeds of the RAF fighter pilots. But the thought that I might some day wear the same uniform and take the battle to Germany never entered my mind. I was entrapped by circumstances. Our local hero - and friend of the family - was Wing Commander Miles Delap, a pre-war officer who was credited with sinking the first U-boat of the war and afterwards won the DFC when his Blenheim squadron was almost completely destroyed trying to stop the German breakthrough in the Battle of France in May, 1940. He had sustained a serious leg injury when baling out of his Blenheim and was given a recuperative posting to Belfast to take over the Air Squadron that had just been set up at Queen's University. As I was already an undergraduate at the University it was inevitable, I suppose, that I would join No. 1 Course.

Queen's University Air Squadron

No. 1 Course - July, 1941

Diplock - Rice - Mooney - O'Callaghan - Dallimore.
Artt - Clarke - Corkey - Purce - Kirkpatrick - King - Howard.
McCrea-McCready-Mrs G. McAlister   Bolster-Mathers-McKelvey.
P/O W.H. McCrea-W/C M.V. Delap,DFC-F/L J.R. Oswald -

Chapter 1

Learning to Fly

The Leaving of Liverpool

Having completed the equivalent of Initial Training at the University Air Squadron I reported for full-time service on 23rd September, 1941, at the Aircrew Reception Centre in London, to join an intake that was almost exclusively from the country's various universities. We were medically examined, inoculated, kitted out, taught how to march, and constantly reminded about the dangers of venereal disease. We ate at Regent's Park Zoo and were paid behind the Mound Stand at Lord's Cricket Ground. Pay for my first two weeks as a humble AC2 was one pound and ten shillings. We were given 'white flashes' for our caps to denote our status as aircrew under training and spent much time in discussion as to when and where such training might begin.

It became reasonably clear that we were bound for the other side of the Atlantic when we were moved to Wilmslow in Cheshire, not far from the port of Liverpool. When we were told to paint the word 'Arnold' on our kitbags general opinion had it that we were bound for the United States. Someone had read somewhere about the Arnold Scheme, under which would-be British aircrew were being taught to fly by the U.S. Army Air Corps. In due course we marched a long two miles with full kit to the railway station and from there to Liverpool docks, to stow our kitbags in the hold of the 'Highland Princess' and to parade with 'small kit' beside the hammocks that were to be our quarters for the ensuing voyage. The 'Highland Princess' had been used for the conveyance of meat from the Argentine. Although the refrigeration equipment had been removed the smell still remained. This was all-pervading and forced all save the most hardy to seek fresher air above decks.

During 1941, the Battle of the Atlantic was reaching a critical phase. German submarines were having marked success against the slow-moving and inadequately protected convoys. As far as I could make out there were twelve ships in our convoy, which was initially under the protection of two destroyer escorts and what appeared to be a makeshift aircraft carrier. The carrier had a complement of two Swordfish aircraft. One of these was seen to flop into the ocean shortly after take-off and when the remaining aircraft failed to return from its reconnaissance mission the carrier fell astern and we saw it no more.

As we left the Irish coast, I looked back wistfully at my home county of Donegal and wondered if I would ever see it again. Shortly afterwards, the need for a protective escort disappeared. Nature took over, and for the next five days the 'Highland Princess' had to endure a Force 10 Atlantic gale. Although we were ordered to stay below decks this proved impossible; the atmosphere became more poisonous day by day. I found some solace and shelter in a corner behind a bulkhead. My shelter was still open to the wind and occasional spray but at least I could breathe fresh air. In my greatcoat and lifebelt I crouched, sick, cold and shivering, for the next two days and nights, scarcely caring whether or not the ship stayed afloat. Indeed, I firmly believed that I had little chance of surviving the crossing.

Thankfully, on the fifth day the wind dropped slightly. A kind pilot officer saw my plight and asked me if I would like to clean the buttons on his uniform. It took at least an hour in his cabin before my hands were warm enough to hold the cleaning materials and I made sure the task lasted through the rest of the afternoon. The officer was also on his way to the United States for flying training but I never found out how he had acquired his commission. Over the next few days I spent a lot of time in his cabin, not cleaning his buttons but just discussing what the future might hold in store for both of us. On occasions I had a doze on his bunk while he went off to his mess for a meal or a drink. Without his kindness I would have taken so much longer to recover.

The storm had left many of the would-be aircrew in very bad shape. The ship's hospital was full to capacity and many who should have been in hospital had to endure the smell and squalor of their accommodation below decks. Eating had been out of the question for most during the storm but warm soup was produced as the wind kept dropping and life aboard gradually became bearable once more.

Eventually complete calm returned to the surface of the ocean and the convoy proceeded slowly towards the New World. As we sailed past the Gulf of St. Lawrence towards our destination, Halifax, the sight was breathtaking. We had arrived at the climax of the North American 'fall'. The splendour of the autumnal colours followed us on our two-day train journey through French Canada and on to Toronto.

We spent seven days in Toronto, first of all recovering from the effects of rich, unrationed food on unaccustomed and empty stomachs and then being kitted out with grey flannel suits for our journey south to a non-combatant United States. Although we were to retain our RAF uniforms we were told that under no circumstances were these to be worn outside military or air force establishments. While in Toronto I found time to visit Niagara Falls and to meet both my uncles, Bill and Jack, who had left Ireland in the twenties to seek their fortunes across the seas. My uncle Bill had certainly succeeded, becoming Vice-President of the Canadian off-shoot of the engineering firm Babcock and Wilcox.

At the end of the week we assembled at the railway station to board the train that would take us to the United States. The sight of seven hundred and fifty British airmen in ill-fitting grey flannel aroused both curiosity and mirth among the many onlookers.

Pilot Training - American Style

Our destination in the United States turned out to be the Reception Centre at Montgomery in Alabama where no one had any difficulty in acclimatising to American food but several found it hard to accept American discipline. The class of 42E, as we were now to be known, contained many ex-policemen who, for the first time, had been allowed to volunteer for flying training. Most of these men had dealt with the aftermath of German attacks on British cities and did not take kindly to the 'West Point' system of punishment under which small misdemeanours would earn penalty points or 'demerits'. Talking on parade, for instance, or smoking in the public areas, would result in five demerits, the maximum allowed in any one week. Any excess over this number would leave the offender marching up and down the parade ground on his day off, one hour for each demerit over the five allowed. On our first day off, or 'open post' in West Point parlance, it came as no surprise when most of those whose names were on the punishment list decided to walk into town rather than march on the parade ground. On the following morning, the entire class was assembled and told by the RAF Exchange Officer that if there was any repetition, those responsible would immediately be despatched to Canada to await shipment back to the United Kingdom where they would face court martial.

Further trouble was averted by our allocation to the various elementary flying schools. I went to Souther Field near Americus, a town in Georgia about 120 miles south of Atlanta. Here we flew the Stearman PT17, a biplane similar to, but more powerful than, the Tiger Moth. All the instruction was given by civilians; most of these men had been crop-dusters or barnstormers who flew by instinct but who now had to absorb and deliver the stereotyped training exercises of the US Army Air Corps. Some tolerance was permitted in the number of hours a trainee took to 'solo' but afterwards standards were rigidly applied by the Army 'check-pilots' and any shortfall resulted in a speedy return to Canada and remustering for training in one of the other aircrew categories.

Nearly all the unskilled staff at Souther Field, such as waiters, shoe-shine boys and cleaners, were coloured and the RAF trainees quickly built up a rapport with these cheerful individuals. But any attempt to talk to them on the streets of Americus was invariably followed by a rebuke from one of the white inhabitants. The harshness of the punishment meted out to coloured offenders could be seen on our frequent route marches along the red earthen roads around Americus when we met the chain gang from the local prison. We could hear them coming, the clanking of their chains mingling with the low chanting of some negro spiritual. We responded immediately with a marching song of our own, bringing it to a crescendo as the two groups met, much to the delight of the prisoners and the obvious disapproval of the attendant warders.

There was very little to do in Americus during our 'open posts' which came around every eight to ten days; most airmen tended to gravitate to the local cinema. It was much too hot for jackets but the grey flannel trousers had been supplemented in most cases by shirts of every colour and design. On one particular evening, when the majority of the cinema audience were clearly identifiable by their dress as RAF trainees, the screen suddenly went blank and the Cinema Manager appeared to announce the Japanese attack on Pearl Harbor. There was much confusion and some tears among the American element of the audience. One group started to sing 'God Bless America' but this attracted little support. After about fifteen minutes the RAF men grew restless and left the manager in no doubt that they wanted the show to continue. After all, they had been at war for more than two years and they told him so. Pearl Harbor had a cataclysmic effect on world events but as far as we were concerned it meant the end of grey flannel trousers and gaudy shirts. We were all issued with

"Off you go". My instructor, Jack Gregg, sends me off for my first solo flight.

1st December, 1941

With Max McCready at Souther Field

attractive khaki shirts and slacks, which were worn both on and off camp during the rest of our training.

Early in January 1942, what was left of Class 42E - about two-thirds of the original number - left Souther Field and moved on to one of the basic flying schools. At a school close to Macon, near the southern extremity of Georgia State, I learned to fly the Vultee BT13 - known also as the 'Yale' - under the guidance of Second Lieutenant Shaw. Johnny Shaw was a most patient man; he had to be for I soon grew to dislike the BT13. I found it unresponsive, particularly during spins and stalls, and the compulsory aerobatics were always completed with great relief. Nevertheless, I managed to put my dislike aside and finished this stage of training in early March.

We were now entitled to a week's leave and five of us from the Air Squadron were invited to spend our leave in Atlanta as the guests of John Harland, whose brother Wallace had been one of the best known Irish rugby referees between the wars. One of the group was Max McCready. We were old friends and had played many games of golf together. We had joined the RAF on the same day, our service numbers were consecutive, and we had been together in training so far. Having arrived in Atlanta our main objective was to visit East Lake, the home course of the immortal Bobby Jones.

I had developed an interest in golf at a very early age and as I grew up I tried all I could to improve my game. But I had no access to a teaching professional and instructional aids were hard to come by. Thankfully, I had been given a set of little booklets known as 'flickers' which, when the pages were run through under one's thumb, showed in simulated motion the swings used by Bobby Jones for his driver, mid-iron, mashie and niblick. The last three of these terms are now obsolete but in the early 1930s Jones' action was the classic example and I used these 'flickers' over and over again until they fell to pieces. Jones had a brilliant career which he crowned in 1930 by winning the Open and Amateur Championships of Britain and

America. After this amazing achievement, which will never be repeated, and with no more fields left to conquer, he retired at the age of twenty-eight. I had wanted to play golf like Bobby Jones. He was my idol and my inspiration and I knew that I must see where he played his golf.

John Harland lost no time in arranging for Max and myself to play at East Lake. To cap it all, the person who would show us around the course would be none other than Charlie Yates, who had won the British Amateur Championship four years before. Before playing, Charlie took us into the Jones Room in the old clubhouse where his many trophies were displayed. We looked at the specially commissioned replicas of his 1930 triumphs and wondered what manner of man could have held all these trophies at the same time.

We enjoyed our round at East Lake. I would like to report that I played well, but indeed I did not. Mercifully, Max was in his normal good form and matched Charlie shot for shot so my lack of skill did not spoil their enjoyment. Max was an exceptionally fine golfer who equalled Charlie Yates' achievement in 1949 when he, too, won the British Amateur Championship, played for the only time outside Britain over the great Portmarnock links near Dublin. As we approached the 16th green a golfer who had been practising his putting stood back to let us play. I paid no attention until Yates shouted, "Bob, you always tell everyone you were born on St. Patrick's Day. Now come and meet a couple of real Irishmen." As Bobby Jones came forward to shake our hands I could scarcely believe what was happening. Not only had I played over his course but now I had met the great man himself. "Come and play the last two holes with us, Bob." said Yates. I had gone through that Jones swing on the 'flickers' thousands of times and now I was to see the real thing. I was surprised that it seemed to be unchanged until I remembered that he was still only 40 years of age.

During the week, John Harland showed us around the beautiful city of Atlanta, including some of the scars left by the Union Forces as they swept through the city on their way to the sea. He also decided to 'show us off' at a civic reception where he introduced us with some pride to many local dignitaries. After talking for several minutes to a charming lady who seemed most interested in our opinion of America, I asked John Harland who she was. "Why, that was Margaret Mitchell," said John. "And what does she do?" He looked at me with pity. "She wrote 'Gone with the Wind'." I did feel rather foolish. After all, this was Atlanta.

Shortly after my 21st birthday I arrived at Napier Field in Dothan, just over the state border in Alabama, to complete my pilot training on the Harvard AT6A. I took to the Harvard at once. It was more sophisticated and more powerful than the Yale. The undercarriage was retractable and consequently the aircraft, being clean, was a joy to fly. The first remarks of my instructor, Lieutenant Delaney, "My grandfather was Irish so we're going to get on just fine," set the pattern for the next six weeks. We had been introduced to night and instrument flying at Basic School but now these became major elements of the curriculum. We flew in two- and three-ship formation and undertook several night cross-countries, using the illuminated airlanes that seemed to stretch across the entire continent.

Off duty, many of the RAF trainees, myself included, made their way to Panama City, a seaside resort on the gulf coast not too far distant from Dothan. My travelling companion was usually Alex McGarvey, a former Glasgow policeman, an excellent swimmer and wrestler who had played water polo for Scotland. The sea and sand provided the relaxation we needed and we returned to camp refreshed to face the final stages of our training. At a ceremonial parade on 16th May, 1942, each survivor of Class 42E was presented with a pair of US Army Air Corps silver wings. At last we had qualified as pilots.

Alex McGarvey

All-in wrestler
Swimmer extraordinary
Stirling Pilot
George Medal

'Beach Bum'

Author relaxing
on the pier,
Panama City

Another long train journey took us north to Moncton, New Brunswick, where we kicked our heels for three weeks waiting to be shipped back to England. Apart from sewing our sergeant's stripes and the treasured RAF wings on our tunics there was nothing to do. Eventually we moved on to Halifax where we boarded the 'Empress of Scotland' and in the cabins that we were now entitled to as senior NCOs enjoyed a calm and trouble-free passage to Liverpool.

From Liverpool another train took us to Bournemouth where we spent a further three weeks in a former sea-front hotel aimlessly marking time until we could commence our operational training. As to whether that would be on fighters or bombers no one knew. The fact that our return to England coincided with the start of the main build-up of the bomber offensive decided our futures. The great bulk of the pilots of Class 42E would be directed towards Bomber Command.

Chapter 2

Learning to Fight

Goosenecks and Goosepimples

We left Bournemouth in July 1942 and moved to No. 3 (Pilot) Advanced Flying Unit at RAF South Cerney in Gloucestershire. There were twenty-four pilots on the course, all products of American training schools. We spent the first two weeks becoming familiar with the Airspeed 'Oxford', the standard twin-engined RAF trainer. At first, I found map-reading difficult as the ground seemed to pass underneath so quickly. This was not because the Oxford was faster than the Harvard; it wasn't. In England, however, towns, roads and rivers were fitted into a much smaller space and, as a result, the countryside below offered up a quite different perspective. The Oxford flew reasonably well on a single engine and we practised all manner of manoeuvres with one engine throttled back. When making a single-engined landing the 'dead' engine was opened up at the point of touchdown. The aircraft simply carried on along the runway and took off on another circuit. I found that this exercise made me nervous as I feared that the 'dead' engine might not respond after it had been idling for several minutes, but thankfully in my case my fears were groundless.

I had little trouble in mastering the Oxford in daylight but night-flying was an entirely different matter. For this we moved to what was known as a relief landing ground at Long Newnton not far from South Cerney. At Long Newnton there were no runways and the landing area was marked with a series of 'goosenecks' - metal canisters filled with paraffin into which a wick had been inserted which, when lit, gave out a yellow flame. Frequently the wind would blow out some of the lights. If too many failed the Airfield Controller in his caravan at the beginning of the flarepath would fire off a red Verey light to keep the pilots airborne until the lighting was restored.

My first experience of night-flying over blacked-out England was a tremendous shock. After the last of the goosenecks had passed beneath us there was only total darkness: no horizon and no lights ahead or below. In America all the towns had been ablaze with lights and the beacons marking the many airlanes were visible for miles. My instructor, Sergeant Bartram, quickly sought to put me at ease by saying, "Keep your eyes on your instruments as soon as you leave the ground. Look at the artificial horizon. Keep the little aircraft above it and the wings level and you'll be fine. You'll start to see more in a few minutes." Sergeant Bartram was right. I soon began to see various lights on the ground. The night was reasonably clear and in the distance I could see two airfields with full permanent lighting. Our goosenecks, a few miles to starboard, looked most insignificant.

I had just started to feel comfortable when Bartram said, "Take her back and land her. It's just the same as in daylight - and you have an approach indicator to help." In truth, I didn't feel quite ready for a night landing but nevertheless I positioned myself on the downwind leg and went through the normal procedures. If it became difficult, I had an instructor beside me. As I turned towards the flickering goosenecks I saw the flash of the controller's green light to indicate that my landing was authorised. I noticed that the approach light to the left of the flarepath was red just about the same time as I heard Bartram's caution, "You're too low. Up a bit." A touch on both throttles and the red light changed to green. "That's fine. Hold it there, and don't put down full flap until you're committed to the landing." My landing evidently pleased Bartram because after we had cleared the goosenecks he said, "Now take-off again and show me a single-engined approach. Break it off at a hundred feet and go round again. I don't ask my pupils to carry out 'touchdown' single-engined landings at night. If you get in the right position at a hundred feet you can land without any engines at all." I was grateful for Bartram's dispensation and after a couple of approaches and a final landing, thankfully on both engines, he said, "Drop me off at the flight hut and take her up for an hour. Do a couple of landings, no single-engine stuff, and have a look round generally. But for heaven's sake, don't get lost." An hour later I got out of the aircraft at dispersal and noticed that I was drenched in sweat. I had been in the aircraft for two hours and I had had to concentrate for every second. There was nothing carefree about flying at night over wartime England.

In the course of the next week I carried out cross-country exercises, usually with another pupil pilot, and finally got around to the dreaded 'overshoot' from the full flap position. All pilots must be prepared to abandon any attempt to land if they find themselves too high on the final approach, or if ordered to do so by Flying Control. This is known as an 'overshoot' and the Oxford called for careful handling in this situation at night. Pilots had to be particularly careful when the full extent of flaps, which had the effect of slowing down the aircraft's speed, had been selected. These had to be 'milked off', little by little, before the Oxford could climb and rejoin the traffic pattern. On my first effort, after I cleared the goosenecks and started to milk off the flaps, I felt that the aircraft was sinking and found it hard to trust my instruments which were telling me that everything was in order. My instructor now was a Flying Officer Wykes, a tall slim chap, prematurely bald with a heavy moustache. After my second overshoot he said, "That's enough. If I were you I would never do this again unless you have to."

Sometimes the weather was against us, even though it was high summer. On this particular night I had been chatting in the flight hut with Sergeant Langridge who was the other pupil pilot assigned to Flying Officer Wykes. I liked Langridge. He had been with me all through training in America and we had helped each other out in ground school on a few occasions. The flying programme had already been postponed for an hour and we were starting to look forward to getting to bed at a reasonable time when Flying Officer Wykes burst into the hut, his parachute over his shoulder. "The Met people have cleared us for flying. They expect the cloud base to lift shortly. Let's do a few landings. No overshoots, I promise you." He looked at Langridge, then at me, then back to Langridge again. "Right, Langridge, I'll take you first. McCrea, be ready for me in about forty minutes." I had just settled down in one of the reasonably comfortable old leather chairs when I heard the screaming protest of an aircraft engine at full revs followed by a loud explosion. By the time I had reached the door of the hut the flames were already being reflected in the low clouds drifting over the airfield. An airman hurried past on his bicycle. I grabbed him and shouted, "What the hell was that?" He shouted back as he rode off, "One of the Oxfords has gone in. I think it was Flying Officer Wykes."

I went back into the hut, sat down at the table and placed my head in my hands. I started to shake, gently at first and then quite violently. My shaking was punctuated by a dash to throw up on the gravel path outside the hut. I was still shaking - and now sobbing - when an officer came in. "Was it Flying Officer Wykes?" I asked. "Yes, it was." "And Langridge?" "Yes. They hadn't a chance. Were you waiting to fly with Wykes?" "Yes, I was. He took Langridge first . I don't know why." The officer came over and put his hand on my shoulder. "You're a lucky fellow, Sergeant. I hope it stays with you. Come on. I'll take you back to South Cerney."

Authors note:
The Air Historical Branch has given me further details about the crash. Apparently, Flying Officer Wykes did not keep his promise to Langridge and myself. He did carry out an overshoot on that fateful night, whether by choice or through necessity we shall never know. The subsequent investigation concluded that 'flying control was lost at 500 feet during an overshoot for reasons which could not be ascertained, and that the instructor was unable to regain control of the aircraft before it hit the ground'.

No. 3 (Pilot) Advanced Training Unit
Long Newton   July 1942

Medland - McCrea - Milligan - Penry - Richardson - Stables - Thomas
Divall - Hartwell - Hawkins - Hirst - Jennings - Jones - Langridge - Mathers
Biggs - Calder - Botham - Cox - Smart - Stuart - Wynn - Fry - Grimwood

Operational Training

My next stop was 29 Operational Training Unit at RAF North Luffenham in Rutland where I joined up with the first members of my crew. Much has been written about the RAF method of 'crewing up'. The various categories were placed together in a large hanger and told to sort themselves into crews. As far as we were concerned, the method worked. First of all, I found my navigator: 'Burma' Gibson impressed me immediately. His nickname came naturally from the land of his birth; he was a much older man - at least 33 years old - and I felt that his calm demeanour and worldly experience would be an asset. He was dark and handsome and together we set about recruiting the other three members of our crew. We found our wireless operator quite quickly; his name was Coxall and he came from the East End of London. He had been christened Ernest but he liked to be known as Joe. We found our bomb-aimer in Vernon Adams, a delightfully loquacious Welshman from the Rhonnda Valley. The rear gunner was the most difficult but in the end we agreed to ask a Canadian, Asa Clark from Moose Jaw in Saskatchewan, to join us. 'Ace' was larger than life, arrogant and confident; we thought that this was just what was needed in a rear gunner.

We spent the next week learning all about each other and trying to shape ourselves into a crew and not just five individuals. We knew that if we did not quickly become an efficient flying and fighting unit we stood little chance of survival. The bonds of friendship quickly developed as we did everything together, both on and off the station; this helped immensely in making us a team, each one dependent on the others. I found the Wellington a much more friendly aircraft than the Oxford; this was hardly suprising in view of my experience at Long Newnton. The first two weeks were spent mainly on take-offs and landings, both day and night. Day cross-countries followed, always culminating in a bombing exercise from either high or low level. When we graduated to the same exercises by night we realised that we were getting near the end of our training.

There was one unpleasant incident. On 27th September we took off on a night cross-country with a staff pilot in charge. Due to a rapid deterioration in weather conditions, we were recalled after little more than an hour in the air. As the pupil I was in the left hand seat and as we approached the vicinity of North Luffenham I noticed a glow outside the aircraft. On looking out of the cockpit I saw flames coming from the port engine. The staff pilot immediately took over control and carried out emergency fire procedures: throttling back, pressing the extinguisher button and 'feathering' the propellor blades. In layman's terms, this last action simply turned the edge of the blades towards the direction of travel, thus reducing the drag. After about a minute, the staff pilot asked me if the flames had gone out. I replied that they were not as bad as they had been but they were still there. This information prompted him to initiate a 'Mayday' call and turn towards a flarepath that had miraculously appeared in front of us. I could even see the green Aldis light being directed at us from the caravan at the end of the flarepath inviting us to make a landing.

Although the staff pilot had completed a tour of operations he appeared to be rather agitated. In truth, he did not handle the situation well; he was too low and the single engine was thrusting the aircraft well clear of the flarepath. I could see the boundary lights pass beneath us and we hit the ground well to the left of the lights. The impact snapped my harness and I felt my face being forced into the instrument panel in front of me. The cockpit filled with dust and debris and I remember thinking 'so this is what an aircraft crash is like'. Happily, the pressure on my body gradually diminished as the aircraft came to rest. I opened the hatch above our heads and we were well clear of the aircraft in a matter of seconds. All of us, that is, except 'Ace' Clarke, our rear gunner, who had some difficulty in leaving his turret. When he did disentangle himself, he stepped out on one of the wing-tips. We had 'arrived' at Woolfox Lodge, a relief landing ground beside the Great North Road, near the famous Ram Jam Inn. We were told afterwards that our port wing had hit the corner of the bomb dump and that if we had been a few yards further left the crash might have had a different ending. I finished up with minor facial scars which stayed throughout my life. These, thankfully, were the only wounds I sustained on active service.

Over the last month of the course we carried out various exercises which were designed to help us blend together as a crew: cross-countries for the navigator and wireless operator, bombing details for the bomb-aimer, and air firing for the gunner, using either live ammunition against towed targets, or the special cine-camera mounted in the turret against simulated attacks from the unit's single-seater 'Master'.

We finished our OTU course in late October, but instead of going to an operational squadron, we moved to a dreary hutted camp at Winthorpe, near Newark, to await a vacancy at a Lancaster Conversion Unit. Here our crew was completed with the addition of Stan Guy, Australian by birth and an ex-RAF engine fitter, who joined us as Flight Engineer. The final crew member was Chris Allen, who became our mid-upper gunner. Chris came from Devon, where his father was Rector of Iddesleigh, not far from Okehampton. This fact pleased my mother immensely, who was convinced that with his background, Chris would keep us all out of trouble. How little she knew.

At Winthorpe the crews from the Operational Training Units were joined by various individuals from the squadrons who, for one reason or another - mainly illness - had lost their places in their original crews and would remain at Winthorpe until vacancies became available. Some of these men, having had experience of operational flying, found it amusing to treat the new boys to various horror stories of what to expect over Germany. The morale of the crews was at a low ebb and the

Commanding Officer did not help. A Scot of World War One vintage, he took great delight in telling his captive audiences in minute detail what the 'Jocks' did to the Germans when they overran their trenches. Eventually our time at this miserable place came to an end. We were sent on Christmas leave with the promise that when we came back we would, at last, be sent to fly Lancasters.

Conversion to Heavies

Immediately after Christmas we were transported the short distance to Swinderby, the home of No. 1660 Conversion Unit. We had our first flight as a seven-man crew on the penultimate day of 1942. Our aircraft was the Avro Manchester which had long since been withdrawn from operational service. Under-powered by two Vulture engines, its low ceiling, poor rate of climb and abysmal performance on one engine had quickly relegated it to a training role. Two hundred had come off the production line and rumour had it that only thirty or so were left.

We tried hard to reduce this number on our final Manchester flight on 13th January. The first two parts of the exercise went well. After the gunners tested their skills against a towed target over the sea off Skegness, we completed a cross-country, arriving back over Skegness at exactly the time estimated. The final part of the exercise was a time-distance run from a point on the coast to the practice range at Wainfleet, there to drop our bombs. But try as we might we could not find the range. The visibility was deteriorating and, after the third abortive attempt, Stan became concerned about one of the engines which he said was overheating. The thought of a single-engine landing was enough to make me turn the aircraft immediatly towards base and set landing procedures into operation.

"Temperature's still going up, Skip." Stan's voice sounded anxious. I looked out and saw some intersecting runways a short distance to port. "OK, Stan. We'll put down over there. Keep an eye on the dodgy engine. If it fails, be ready to feather the props immediately." Using the emergency frequency, we obtained permission to land and after a normal circuit I made what I considered to be a very good landing. As I throttled back and ran along the runway, I congratulated myself in getting out of what might have been a difficult situation. This self-congratulation, however, was very much premature. Approaching the end of the runway I applied the brakes so that I could turn off onto the perimeter track. Nothing happened and repeated applications had the same result. Mindful of warnings about the weakness of the Manchester undercarriage, a turn at speed onto the perimeter was not an option. The aircraft left the end of the runway, lurched over the grass and quickly came to a stop, settling perceptibly into the soft earth. It soon became obvious that we could move no further without assistance so we shut off the engines and waited.

A staff car was the first arrival, out of which catapulted a wing commander, his face crimson with rage. "What the hell do you think you are doing? My squadron is taking off on operations tonight and you've blocked the damn runway." "I'm sorry, Sir. We had to land here as one of our engines was overheating and after we landed the brakes failed." The wing commander wasn't listening. He called to a warrant officer who had appeared. "Get spades for these fools." He turned to me. " You have one hour to get this monstrosity clear of the runway. If you don't, you will answer personally to the Commander-in-Chief for preventing a whole squadron taking off on operations. Now get to work." Before the spades had time to arrive a tractor appeared and pulled the Manchester clear in a few minutes.

Airfield Control at Wickenby, for this is where we had landed, had already told Swinderby of our 'safe' arrival. We were to stay overnight and two engineers were to come over in the morning to check that the engine was fit for the return flight. Needless to say, the administrative staff regarded us as unwelcome intruders and told us so. We were given a quite inedible meal in an annex to the Sergeants' Mess; we could not use the public rooms as we were still wearing flying gear. Eventually, we were told that we could use the beds set aside for a new crew which was due to arrive the following morning. The Nissen hut that was to be our home for the night was the most depressing we had ever seen. The single stove in the middle of the hut polluting the air with coke fumes was obviously not enough to prevent the growth of the white mould that covered most of the walls. Seven of the beds were made up. The personal effects scattered around suggested that the crew was among those taking off along the runway now clear of encumbrances. On each of the unoccupied beds were three biscuits, two coarse blankets and a pillow. All were damp to the touch and the smell was no more inviting. That night all of us slept in our flying clothing.

One intriguing feature of the hut was the collection of lavatory chains - some thirty or forty of them - that hung over the occupied beds. Apparently these had been collected from the various pubs that the crew had visited. This was our introduction to an operational station and we found it upsetting. Surely bomber aircrew, risking their lives night after night, deserved better. We barely noticed the safe return of those who shared our hut. There seemed to be little reaction to the raid they had just carried out. They spoke little, fell into their beds and were soon asleep. This was not at all what we imagined life to be like on an operational squadron.

We flew our Manchester back to Swinderby next morning and the following day had our introduction to the Avro Lancaster. For me, it was an unforgettable experiece. The designer, Roy Chadwick, bitterly disappointed by the failure of the Manchester, had increased its wingspan and replaced the two Vulture engines with four Rolls-Royce Merlins. The result was one of the greatest aircraft in the history of air warfare. The Lancaster was a dream to fly. Immediately responsive to the pilot's instructions, it had no vices. Although night landings were normally made using some power from the engines, most pilots, during daylight, executed a 'three-pointer', with the main wheels and tail wheel touching simultaneously, with no more difficulty than they had experienced in an elementary trainer. I was delighted to make my first solo flight in the aircraft in which Wing Commander John Nettleton won his Victoria Cross over Augsburg in April 1942.

One disturbing feature of our time at Swinderby was the developing animosity directed by Ace Clarke, our rear gunner, towards Chris Allen, our mid-upper, who had joined the crew at Winthorpe. Ace was openly critical of 'the ex-public schoolboy with the long hair and posh accent'. This ill-feeling had an effect on our social activities; if one gunner was to be in the group, the other sought his pleasure elsewhere. In the air there was no problem. They worked well as a team and, indeed, were largely responsible for our good results in the end-of-course tests, which affected our final assessment. We were examined in airmanship, in dingy drill, in aircraft recognition, and our two gunners were tested on the rifle range and on clay pigeons. Chris had had plenty of rifle practice in the Officer Training Corps at his public school, St. John's, Leatherhead, and as clay pigeon shooting was a universal pastime in his native Devon, he had little difficulty in achieving a near-maximum in both disciplines. Ace's score fell a long way short, a result which added more fuel to the smouldering fire, but together the scores achieved by our gunners took us up to first place. Our achievement was received with disbelief by a squadron leader who, with his experienced crew, was converting to Lancasters prior to starting a second tour.

On completion of our course at Swinderby we waited with fingers crossed as posting time approached. After our depressing experience at Wickenby we were fervently hoping

for a squadron on a peace-time station. To our relief, we were
posted to No 57 Squadron at RAF Scampton.

John Greenan and his crew before take-off.
RAF Scampton.

Scampton Churchyard. Journey's End.

Gentlemen. Your target for tonight is Berlin.

Waiting for the bus. Note the wireless operator with his
carrier pigeons(W)

Chapter 3

Gently Does It

Welcome to the Squadron

The RAF station at Scampton lay a few miles north of the city of Lincoln. We arrived there early in February 1943 and liked what we saw. The Sergeants' Mess was large and comfortable, quite unlike anything we had to put up with during training. The NCOs of each crew were accommodated in what were formerly married airmen's quarters, one crew to each quarter, which now provided three bedrooms as well as a bathroom and kitchen. Of course, there were not enough of these quarters to go round and new crews had to wait their turn in one of the large wooden huts near the Mess. Sadly, many of the new arrivals did not survive long enough to qualify for the more up-market accommodation.

At last we came to the head of the queue. On 2nd March the Station Warrant Officer (SWO) burst into the hut as we were dressing for breakfast, called out my name and told me that we could move into a quarter of our own that afternoon. "Just one thing," said the SWO, "The crew living there before you were all killed in a crash last night. There will be a military funeral and you lot have been detailed as pall-bearers."

During the morning there were all kinds of rumours about the crash, very few of them bearing any resemblance to the truth. We knew that Flying Officer Greenan and his crew had been posted missing after the raid on Berlin. We were sorry to hear this as we had had a few drinks in the Mess a couple of nights previously with the NCOs in Greenan's crew and they had seemed 'a pleasant lot of bods', to use the RAF slang of the period. What actually happened was later written about at length. A Lancaster from 9 Squadron, preparing to land at Waddington, south of Lincoln, was involved in a head-on collision with Greenan's Lancaster from Scampton. The New Zealand pilot of the Waddington aircraft, Jim Verran, together with three members of his crew, miraculously survived, but the 57 Squadron Lancaster, although it managed to stay airborne for some minutes, eventually hit some power cables and crashed in flames. Greenan and his crew all perished.

Six members of the Greenan crew were to be buried in the churchyard in the village that gave the airfield its name. The pall-bearers were paraded outside the station mortuary and meticulously inspected by the Station Warrant Officer. They were then sorted into groups of six according to height and given explicit instructions as to how the coffins should be carried. The coffins, each draped with the appropriate flag, were placed on a 'low-loader' which set off for the churchyard followed by the marching pall-bearers. At the churchyard gates the groups stepped forward, one after the other, to lift the coffins and carry them on their last journey to six newly-dug graves.

After the burial service, conducted by the Station Padre, the pall-bearers were called to attention and six airmen from the RAF Regiment fired a volley over the graves. It was indeed a sombre occasion and I began to worry about the effect it might have on myself and my crew. We had, after all, only started our tour and had not yet flown as a crew against a German target. I felt that we should not have been detailed for this particular duty so soon after joining the squadron. I was rash enough to say so to the Station Warrant Officer later in the day and had immediate regrets when I heard his answer. " There were only bodies in four of the coffins, the other two were filled with sand. If you believe that you carried one of these you'll feel better." I found his remarks in the worst possible taste but I later discovered that they were quite out of character. He really was a fine Station Warrant Officer who did all he could to make the lives of the NCO aircrew as comfortable as possible. It was only when I stopped and talked to him one day after I had been commissioned that I discovered that his son was also flying on operations.

I had already had my first experience of operations when on 19th February I flew as second pilot to Sergeant Paul Hawkins on a raid against Wilhelmshaven. Some two weeks later we carried out our first operation as a crew against the submarine pens at St. Nazaire. Now that we had moved into proper accommodation we felt like permanent members of the squadron and ready for everything that was to come. We remained on 57 Squadron until we completed our tour on the 18th October. Many of our operations were without incident. Apart from the continual and fearful apprehension of waiting for something to happen they could almost be described as boring. Any crew that experienced thirty such trips was indeed fortunate. On the ensuing pages I have described only unusual incidents as well as those trips on which something out of the ordinary happened. Almost half the raids in which we were involved came into this category.

The Ides of March

It was the 15th of March. The aircrews had reported to the squadron crew-room at 09:30 hours as usual. Two small groups were playing cards, others were reading the morning newspapers, some were talking and a few were just sitting quietly, looking at nothing in particular. There was no point in looking out of the window, the morning fog was intense. The aircraft had been parked the previous evening, one behind the other on the perimeter track waiting for take-off instructions that never came. Another 'scrub' - they seemed to be all too frequent these days. Abandoned sorties meant a lot of extra work for the armourers. Instead of returning to dispersal after the cancellation, the aircraft were sometimes left where they were, to be disarmed next day.

The sound of the explosion was preceded fractionally by the blast that removed the glass in the crew-room windows and deposited it in fragments over the aircrew inside. Confusion reigned. One of the gunners was bleeding badly from a cut on his cheek but otherwise no one seemed injured. The Squadron Commander's voice came over the tannoy: "All 57 pilots report to their own aircraft immediately. At the double..Go...Go." Having just returned from leave on the previous evening I had no aircraft to go to but I set off to see if I could help. I ran across the perimeter track and past Flying Control in the general direction of the parked aircraft. The visibility was no more than ten yards; I had little idea where I was going. I sensed the second explosion before the sound reached me. The blast had perceptibly caused the fog to move. I headed towards the source of the noise but when I arrived back at Flying Control some minutes later I realised that I had no chance of finding the aircraft. The explosions, although somewhat muffled, were now more frequent so I decided to return to the crew-room. We learned later that morning that only the CO and one other pilot had succeded in reaching and moving their aircraft.

All pilots were summoned and told to inform their crews that the morning's events were not to be discussed, particularly off the station. Rumours were rife throughout the day; the consensus was that an armourer had dropped a photoflash[1] when removing it from the flare-chute, setting off a chain reaction among the parked aircraft. These included one or two that were on loan from other squadrons. Joe's WAAF girlfriend, Edna, who worked in Intelligence, overheard the Squadron Commander, Freddie Hopcroft, responding to the CO of another squadron asking for the return of his aircraft. Freddie's reply was short and to the point: "Bring a brush and dustpan and you can help yourself." The squadron

---

1   Over the target the 'photoflash' was released at the same time as the first bomb. It exploded 30 seconds later, thereby providing the light that enabled the aircraft's camera to photograph the point of impact.

immediately became non-operational and other squadrons in the group were ordered to make their surplus aircraft available. This decision was to have a serious effect on the fortunes of myself and my crew a few weeks later. We would do well to heed the words of the soothsayer in 'Julius Caesar' to 'beware the Ides of March'.

Bomb Disposal

On 22nd March our target was, once again, the submarine pens in the French port of St. Nazaire, on that country's Atlantic coast. We had already been to St. Nazaire on the last day of February and dropped our 4,000lb. 'cookie' right on the aiming point. This is what our target photograph showed and it earned each crew member an 'aiming point certificate'. As this was our first operation as a crew over enemy territory we felt quite proud, even more so when the Squadron Commander singled us out for special mention at briefing. Other photographs were less pleasing, however, to Bomber Command. They showed that the 'cookies' we had dropped had done little damage to the reinforced shields protecting the pens so tonight the bomb load would be changed: each Lancaster would carry ten 1,000lb. armour piercing bombs. We were also informed that, if intelligence reports were to be believed, Goering's favourite squadron of ME109s had been moved to the St. Nazaire area to provide additional protection. The spinners of these aircraft had been painted bright yellow but the Squadron Commander was quick to point out that, even with their yellow-nosed seal of Goering's approval, they were essentially day fighters with no experience against night bombers and their wide-awake gunners.

We had no trouble in finding the target; St. Nazaire was well alight by the time we arrived. As we made our bombing run, Chris in his mid-upper turret fired 120 rounds at an ME110 that was coming in much too close. The night fighter passed through his trace but there was no sign that it had been damaged. A few minutes later, he was warning us, with some

Aiming Point Certificate
St. Nazaire
28th February, 1943

excitement in his voice, that one of the infamous ME109s had passed by a short distance to starboard. We tried to tell him afterwards that the 'yellow nose' was no more than the reflection of the fires below but he would have none of it. Whatever the aircraft was, we didn't attract its attention and we were soon clear of the target and on the way home.

As we crossed the English coast on the return journey, it was becoming clear that by far the most dangerous part of the operation could well be ahead of us. We had not long left the target when we received a signal that Scampton had closed down due to dense fog. We had been given diversion instructions, first of all to airfields in East Anglia, and then in Yorkshire, but soon we were told that in these areas, too, the fog had made landing impossible. Now we were "to continue on course and await instructions." During the next half-hour, I asked Joe Coxall, our wireless operator, at least twice if he was sure that his set was working. He kept assuring me that it was. We were within twenty minutes of base when the message I was dreading came through: "All airfields east of two degrees west closed. Land where you can." Like most young pilots I had been regaled with horror stories about what happened on previous occasions when returning bombers found the whole country covered in thick fog. Some crews baled out over their bases and several aircraft either crashed or were badly damaged when attempting to land on strange airfields. One crew survived after landing on the Great North Road. I could be forgiven for thinking that this could well be a night of similar disasters.

I had also been told that the pilot of one of the aircraft caught out by the fog had landed in Dublin, where the crew had been treated like heroes before the aircraft was refuelled and flown back to England apparently without being noticed by the German Ambassador or any of his staff. As an Irishman I could not imagine a better solution. If we could find a suitable airfield on the way, we would land there; if not, we would press on across the Irish Sea. I asked Burma to give me a course for

Dublin and this was passed to me almost immediately. He told me later that he had expected my request.

As 'D' - Dog flew ever further westwards there was nothing underneath but impenetrable blackness. Then quite suddenly, the cloud cleared and we saw below the most welcoming sight - an airfield with full lighting, its beacon stabbing identifying letters into the night. I made a slow descent around the airfield and noticed that most of the time we were over water. "I've checked the beacon signal," said Burma. "We're over RAF Valley on the Isle of Anglesey." "Skipper here. Does anyone know what Valley is being used for?" There was no answer. I switched to the emergency frequency: "Mayday, Mayday, Valley control from 'D'- Dog. We need to land. Can you take a Lancaster?" The reply sounded like sweet music to my ears. "'D' - Dog from Valley control. Land when you are ready. Approach from the west. You're on our long runway. There's plenty of room."

The landing was not the best I had ever made but we were down in one piece. We were met by a van with a 'Follow Me' sign which led us to a nearby dispersal. After asking Control to inform Scampton of our safe arrival we were soon tucking into a meal of bacon, sausages and beans with mugs of hot tea. "Sorry we have no eggs but we're not an operational station."

Next morning we awoke to clear skies and after a quick breakfast we asked for transport to take us to 'D' - Dog. Everyone piled aboard and we set off across the airfield. Suddenly the vehicle screeched to a halt and two RAF policemen appeared at the rear end. "Are you the aircrew from the Lancaster?" "Yes, I'm the pilot. What's the trouble?" "There's an unexploded bomb jammed between your bomb doors. We have orders to keep everyone clear." "At least, let me have a look," I said. One policeman looked at the other. "Well, it's your responsibility, I suppose, but if anything happens you will have to carry the can."

As I walked under 'D' - Dog and looked up I could see what had happened. The release mechanism on one of the bombs had not functioned properly and it had remained on its rack after I had closed the bomb doors. Subsequently, either sometime on the return journey or, more likely, as we landed it had fallen into the bomb bay. It was now lying at an angle across the doors, which had been forced open leaving a gap of some eight or nine inches. The Station Armament Officer was already at the aircraft. " Have you anyone who can handle this?" I asked. "Not a chance" was the reply. "You will need special tackle and it looks like a job for an expert. You'll have to contact your squadron and get an armament team sent down here."

The bomb looked firmly wedged and I figured that as it hadn't gone off on landing it was not likely to do so if I took the aircraft off again. A squadron leader drove up in a staff car. I saluted and said, "We seem to be causing you some trouble, Sir." "You certainly are. We've been through to Scampton. The lifting tackle would have to come down by road and might not be here for a couple of days but they have asked us to have another look at the situation." "Well, Sir, I'm willing to take the aircraft off and open the bomb doors over the sea. That should get rid of it." The squadron leader was quiet for a few moments. "Are you happy to do that, Sergeant?" "Sir, I hit the runway pretty hard last night and nothing happened. Take-off in a Lancaster is a gentle affair, particularly when it's empty." "O.K. I'll send a fuel bowser out and when you're ready go to the end of the main runway. We'll give you a green light from control when it's clear for you to take off."

After what seemed an interminable wait on the end of the runway a green Aldis lamp flashed out from one of the windows in the control tower. I released the brakes and opened the throttles, slowly at first and then more quickly to maximum power. As 'D' - Dog lifted off the runway, left the airfield behind and headed out to sea. I felt a great sense of relief. Now all I had to do was to find a suitable expanse of sea in which to dispose of our rogue bomb. I flew westwards for ten minutes, climbed to 2,000 feet and did a 360 degree turn in each direction to ensure as far a possible that there were no ships below. As I opened the bomb doors the aircraft juddered as its unwelcome cargo scraped clear. Although several pairs of eyes were focused on the sea below, we saw no sign of our bomb. Certainly it did not explode.

The trip to base was completed without further incident. I had time to reflect on my decision to take off from Valley and decided not to include details of 'the bomb' in my report. I would answer questions, of course, if these were asked. Thankfully, they were not.

On several occasions in later years I tried to convince myself that my take-off from Valley with a fused bomb loose in the bomb bay was anything other than utter stupidity. I failed every time. In theory, as the bomb was fused any slight movement or change of position would have been enough to set it off. I tried to find a reason for my stupidity and came to the conclusion that it was all about degrees of risk. When one has been faced with flak and fighters, including Goering's favourite 'yellow-nosed' ME109s, and then with a perhaps more dangerous battle against encroaching fog, the risk of blowing oneself up with a friendly bomb when taking off from a friendly airfield must have seemed very remote indeed. But risk there certainly was. I should not have taken off until the bomb had been removed by those who had been trained for such tasks.

Others were also to blame. The Senior Officer at RAF Valley should , without doubt, have grounded my aircraft and my squadron at Scampton should also have ordered me to stay put. In retrospect, I feel that both parties were, like me, looking for the simplest and easiest solution. Subsequent events indicated that the bomb might not have been fused, or it might even have been a dud, but this was not known when I took off.

Sadly, I was not able to enjoy my trip to Dublin until after the war. By that time, my method of bomb disposal was a distant, even if always a chastening memory.

Germany at Last

The 'A' Flight Commander, Squadron Leader George Curry, DFC, was particularly good with new arrivals. He believed in breaking them in gently. We had been on the squadron for almost two months and all we had to show were two trips to St. Nazaire and a mine drop off the Frisian Islands. On 29th March he called me to his office and asked if I had any problems. He said he knew that our practice bombing results were good but what about the rest? How was my navigator performing, did my gunners check their guns and turrets regularly, how many dinghy drills had we carried out in the past month? Clearly satisfied with my answers, he said, "I'm putting you on the battle order tonight. It will be your first German target so make a good job of it." As I left his office my feelings were mixed. We were going to bomb Germany and I felt a sense of achievement. This, after all, was the object of all those long months of training. On the other hand, a German target would be quite different from a 'tip-and-run' raid on St. Nazaire. We would have to deal with the formidable strength of the home defences, something we had not yet experienced, and I wondered how we, as a crew, would react.

When I entered the briefing room and looked towards the large map which showed the route to and from the target I caught my breath. Our first German target was to be the big city itself - Berlin. We took seven hours and thirty minutes to drop one 4,000 lb. 'cookie' and twelve containers of incendiaries on the German capital. Over the city, our gunners fired 200 rounds each at three Ju88s which behaved as if they were preparing to attack. Our pre-emptive strike, together with some rather violent evasive action, convinced them that we were not the easy target that they were looking for and we saw no more of them. Otherwise, our first trip to Germany was without incident as was our second five days later, on my 22nd birthday. This time we went to 'Happy Valley', as the Ruhr was known to aircrew, to Essen, where that most heavily defended of German towns lived up to the lurid accounts of the 'old lags[2]'. We were troubled neither by flak, nor searchlights, nor fighters. We flew to the target, dropped our bombs and returned home.

On reflection, the relative lack of incident during these early operations may well have helped us through our tour. The highest casualty rate among RAF bomber aircrew was from those who had completed fewer than five trips. We were now past this mark and mainly through good fortune we had kept clear of trouble. Each member of the crew was becoming more experienced and more confident. We were blending together well, I knew that, but I felt that we could not keep clear of German defences for much longer. Coming events showed that my pessimism was well founded.

2   The C-in-C often referred to his aircrew as 'old lags'.

Chapter 4

Destiny

The 10th of April had started badly - and it was getting worse. Stan's voice came over the intercom, "It's no go Skip. Pressure on the starboard outer is right off the clock." "Are you sure, Stan?" "It's gone sure enough, Skip, I can see the oil on the cowling." So that's it, then - another early return - this time two nights in a row. The previous night had been bad enough: that was the second time in our first half-dozen trips and there had been one or two snide remarks in the mess. Early returns were such a waste. That terrible gut-wrenching wait between briefing and take-off had all been for nothing. If we had reached our target, dropped our bombs and made it back, we would have been one trip closer to the impossible dream - end of tour.

That morning I had been walking to the squadron offices thinking of nothing in particular when the voice boomed out, "Sergeant, come here." I had clearly walked past an officer without saluting. I knew immediately by the three bands on his sleeve and the many DSOs and DFCs on his chest that my indiscipline was serious. My first meeting with Guy Gibson was not a happy one. The only consolation was the black labrador that nuzzled my hand as I bought it down to my side after my belated salute. "Come here, Nigger," said Gibson. "And you, Sergeant, don't you usually salute an officer?" "I'm sorry, Sir, I didn't see you." Gibson snorted, "Are you an operational pilot?" I told him that I was. "How do you expect to survive if you can't keep your wits about you?" I wanted to tell him that I wasn't on ops at the moment but one didn't bandy words with the CO of 617 Squadron. Another apology and another salute and I was on my way.

"Navigator here, Skip. Your course for base is 282." My decision was immediate. This was no time for a consensus of the crew's opinions; the decision had to be mine and mine alone. "Captain to crew. You all know about the engine loss but tonight we are not turning back. We have reached operational height so it is downhill all the way to the target. There are two more waves behind us so these aircraft will give us cover if we are late on target - as we certainly will be. Navigator, knock ten knots off our airspeed and let me have a new ETA (Estimated Time of Arrival). Engineer, keep a close watch on fuel distribution - you know what to do - and let me know if there is any sign of another engine misbehaving."

I could just see the Lincolnshire coast pass below in the darkness. "Gunners, test your guns and report." I felt, rather than heard, the burst from the four Brownings and then the rear gunner's assurance, "OK, Skip." After another, lesser burst of fire, the report from Chris, the other gunner, was less re-assuring: "Mid-upper gunner here, Skip. My hydraulics have gone but I can work the turret by hand and my guns are OK." This sounded like the usual confident Chris but better make sure. "Can you cope, Chris? We'll need you. Can you give us full cover?" The reply sounded cheerful enough, "OK, Skip. No problem."

Half an hour later the navigator sounded apprehensive, "I've got a good fix, Skip. We're on course but we've lost ten minutes." This meant that we were only half-way across the North Sea and already with the second wave of the attack. "Thanks, Burma. Get another fix when we reach the Dutch coast and I'll review the situation." The Dutch coast was always well defended. The first indications were the searchlights, weaving across the night sky attempting to pick out aircraft at random. There was also the ubiquitous flak and many 'free-range' night -fighters flying with the bomber stream looking for opportunity targets.

Thankfully, we avoided the coastal searchlights and as we left the coast behind it was the gunners' turn to be vigilant. We were now entering the night-fighter defence belt which was divided into a series of control boxes. Each box was patrolled by a night fighter which was vectored on to a specific aircraft acquired by ground radar. Once contact was established, the fighter switched on its own airborne radar and was left to pursue the most effective form of attack. The main defence against the ground-controlled fighter was to stay with the bomber stream. Those aircraft that had drifted off course stood out clearly on the radar screens and became easy targets. But night-fighters could be encountered at any time and the best defence of all was without doubt the 'corkscrew'. A gentle dive to starboard was followed by a dive to port, then a climb to starboard and a climb to port. In theory , the manoeuvre was designed to make it difficult for the fighter to line up his sights before firing but many pilots, of whom I was one, believed that if the fighter saw his intended target taking what looked like evasive action, he would decide not to attack and look for another bomber flying straight and level. There was no sentiment in the bomber war; it was every man for himself. Pilots were recommended to carry out the corkscrew manoeuvre every ten minutes or so but this was never enough for me. On every one of my trips I corkscrewed continuously all the time that I was over enemy territory, with the sole exception of the bombing run. Our crew gained a reputation for this eccentricity on the squadron and some even scoffed openly at our timidity. Although some of the crew became airsick from the continuous movement, they were all supportive of my approach. They believed, as I did, that it was the best protection against fighter attack.

As we carried on towards the target, I glanced repeatedly at the feathered blades in front of the useless starboard engine and the reality of our situation - and my decision - became more apparent. If we lost another engine now, either through failure or enemy action we would have to turn back and a lone Lancaster with half its engines gone would be easy prey for predators still lurking in the night-fighter belt. We had to stay with the bomber stream but I had not felt any of the usual turbulence for some time - an indication that we were losing touch. "Skipper to Navigator. Any update on ETA?" "Burma here, Skipper. I've had a good GEE fix. At this rate we'll miss the last wave." We had lost nearly one thousand feet since leaving England, mainly through the asymmetric pull of the engines during the corkscrew, but this was less important than the loss of time. "Skipper to Navigator. We must increase speed. I'll be going downhill all the way to the target. We'll probably lose another thousand feet. And, Bomb-aimer, get those bombs away first time."

It was clear as we approached Frankfurt that the early waves of bombers had completed their attacks. The city was well alight - a mass of red and green markers spluttering throughout huge areas of fire and smoke. Occasional photo-flashes showed that some bombers were still over target. A lone bomber was caught in searchlights a short distance to port. I watched, to my great delight, an attacking fighter come within the lethal range of the rear gunner's 303s and fall away trailing flames. "Bombs gone, Skip." "Thanks, Taff. Bomb doors closed." Now those hellish thirty seconds. Straight and level. Right over the bloody target. Just to take a flaming photograph. But we had to bring one back, especially tonight, just to prove we had been here. The thirty-second light flashed beneath my feet. Before it had gone out, I had pushed the control coumn forward and we were leaving the target area as fast as possible. I saw an area of the city that had not been attacked and headed for that. With no fires beneath us we would have a much better chance and in a few minutes we would have some protection from the darkness.

---

1   GEE - navigational device used to fix aircraft's position.

We left the fires of Frankfurt behind and commenced the long journey home. I did not feel at all comfortable. After an hour's flying the navigator was still unable to obtain a fix and, even with the loss of our bomb load, we were having difficulty in maintaining altitude. We were lost and, worse still, we were alone. We had to get rid of some more weight so I opened the bomb doors and jettisoned the SBCs (small bomb containers). These were normally brought back to be used again but tonight they were expendable. "Skip here, Burma. Keep trying for that fix. We must know where we are. And try as hard as you can because the sky is getting lighter and it will soon be daylight."

Then, in answer to my silent prayer, a chance to make it home. A huge bank of cloud, just a few hundred feet below. I took the aircraft down to the cloud tops. At least we were now safe from fighters attacking from below. "Navigator to Skipper. I've got a fix - not a very good one - but if it's right we will be over the Channel in four minutes." The Channel. Where on earth had we been? I pushed the control column forward and started to descend through the cloud. Almost immediately the aircraft lurched; the cloud grew darker and there were black streaks on the front panel. From down below some AA battery was coming close. Time for evasive action so I dived steeply to starboard. As we broke cloud it was still half-light; above the cloud it had been almost daylight. I saw the coast ahead and kept on diving. If we had to come down in the Channel, there was some chance of our own chaps picking us up. "Captain to Wireless Operator. Get ready to send out a 'Mayday' but don't transmit until I tell you to. Gunners, keep your eyes open and if you see anything, start shooting. We only need another ten minutes."

About an hour later we blasted over our empty dispersal on 'A' Flight at a forbidden height just to let our ground crew know that we were back. I hoped that I wouldn't be in trouble for such an arrival. After handing over the aircraft to a relieved ground crew we made our way to the crew room. I made no apology for pushing aside the two airmen who had opened our lockers and were putting our personal possessions into a kitbag. Someone hadn't wasted much time in writing us off. We had to hang around until an Intelligence Officer could be found to carry out de-briefing. As I waited I looked up at the Operations Board and read 'NO WORD' against our aircraft. It was a strange sensation. There was a civilian chap there who seemed very interested in the fact that we had gone all the way to the target and back again on three engines. It turned out that he was a reporter from a national daily and next day we got a mention in the newspapers.

I was awakened by one of the corporals from the squadron orderly room. "The CO wants to see you at once. I'll tell him you'll be there in twenty minutes." Wing Commander Campbell Hopcroft, DFC, had just taken delivery of a new Lancaster, ED989. This was his third, and the name 'FREDERICK III' had already been painted on the aircraft's side together with the usual caricature of himself holding his nose and releasing a bomb on the enemy below. He always flew in 'F' - Freddie and consequently his crews knew him by this name. Freddie was a hard man. No 'milk runs' for him; if he was flying on operations you could bet on a tough target. I knew I shouldn't have beaten up the dispersal but he must be pleased that we didn't turn back. Freddie didn't even mention the 'beat up', but he told me, in no uncertain terms, what he thought about our efforts on the previous night. "I've read your de-briefing report. Why did you not return to base when you lost an engine?" "Sir," I tried to sound plaintive, "We had an early return the night before." "So?" said Freddie, with a lift of his eyebrows. I hesitated and then went on, "Two nights in a row are too many. People talk." The eyebrows came down. "So people talk, do they? Well, I'll talk and you listen. I don't mind about your miserable skin, but if you ever again risk a valuable aircraft and six highly trained aircrew on a damnfool stunt like last night, you'll be off my squadron before you can draw breath. You were lucky to get back. You don't even know where you had been. Neither do we. The Navigation Leader tells me he tried to back-plot your trip but your navigator hadn't kept a log. I'm told he has done this before so I'm asking the Nav Leader to keep a close eye on him. Now get out of my sight." I saluted in silence and turned towards the door. "On second thoughts," roared Freddie, "I can't stand you on the station. I'm bringing forward your leave. When you get back we'll see if you can behave more responsibly."

About ten days later I was having a beer in the Mess when 'Chiefy' Powell from 617 Squadron came up and said, "Wing Commander Hopcroft's office, ten hundred hours tomorrow, best blue." To be on the safe side I got to the squadron orderly room with time to spare. There were three other pilots already there looking awkward in pressed trousers and polished buttons: Geoff Rice, Johnny Divall, and one other I didn't recognise. "What's up?" No one knew.

There were four people behind Freddie's desk. Freddie himself was sitting at one end and the officer conducting the interview was none other than Guy Gibson. A flight lieutenant appeared ready to take notes and opposite Freddie sat a man in civilian clothes who seemed bored with the whole proceedings. "This is Sergeant McCrea," said Freddie. "We've already met," said Gibson, although there was a suspicion of a smile on his face. I suddenly realised what it was all about: he wanted more crews for his new squadron. I didn't take in everything he said but I remember being asked what I thought about low-level attacks at night. And then the question I had been expecting: "What would you do if you lost an engine on the way to the target?" I glanced at Freddie and took a deep breath, "If I was over enemy territory I would press on, Sir." "Did I know of a reason why my crew might not fit in?" Before I could answer the officer taking notes said, "You have had some trouble with your navigator. Has that been sorted?" " I hope so, Sir." I knew immediately that my answer was not positive enough. The ensuing silence indicated a sudden loss of interest and at that point my transfer to 617 Squadron ceased to be a possibility. Geoff Rice and Johnny Divall were both transferred. Geoff went on the Dams Raid and lost his bomb when he flew too low and hit the sea. I often wonder what would have happened to me if Burma had filled in his navigator's log.

Chapter 5

Baltic Adventure

I had no idea what to expect when I was summoned to the squadron commander's office on 28th April. Freddie Hopcroft was seated behind his desk; Squadron Leader Leland, the newly-appointed 'A' Flight Commander, was standing at the window, staring idly at an aircraft taxying past. "Come in and sit down, McCrea." On this occasion, at least, Freddie sounded affable. "We have a special trip for you tonight but we're rather concerned about your navigator. Your Flight Commander has spoken with the Navigation Leader who is not convinced that Gibson can manage. What do you think? If you're not happy we can give you a new navigator." We had not flown since our round trip on three engines to Frankfurt but I had no hesitation in answering the CO's question. "We'll stick with Gibson, Sir. I'm sure he won't let us down." "Good. I expected you to say that. You've already laid some mines off the Frisian Islands but I want you to go a bit further tonight and drop some vegetables in Lubeck Bay. Squadron Leader Leland will arrange a full briefing."

Most crews expected to be sent on one 'gardening' sortie but here we were collecting a second and I wondered why. I heard myself saying, "May I ask a question, Sir?" "Yes, go on," said Freddie. "Is this the trip that Flight Sergeant Mackenzie was sent on last week?" Freddie ceased being affable. "No, it isn't. He was supposed to be going further east to Rostock. And what do you know about Mackenzie?" "Nothing, Sir, except I know that he didn't come back." Based on the facts, I suppose I was speaking the truth but there had been a lot of rumours which must have reached the ears of the Squadron Commander. Mackenzie (for obvious reasons, not his real name) and his crew had been in trouble since their arrival on the squadron. Quite early on, a police van brought them back to the station after an unsavoury incident in a Lincoln hostelry. They made few friends in the Sergeants' Mess, where they drank in isolation and became more rowdy and objectionable as the evening wore on. After one of these drinking bouts, an RAF police sergeant was found unconscious outside the Mess. He had been badly beaten and there was little doubt who had been responsible. Shortly afterwards, however, the police sergeant had his revenge when, called in to investigate a theft from the sergeants' bar, he found the stolen bottles in the rooms occupied by Mackenzie's crew. He passed details to his superiors at Group Headquaters, thus ensuring that the matter could not be dealt with on the station. A 'Summary of Evidence' had been taken and, according to reports, a Court Martial was expected. Until that decision was taken, however, the crew remained operational and in mid-April they were sent to lay mines in the Baltic off Rostock, an operation from which they did not return.

Next day it came out that Mackenzie's rear gunner had told one of the armourers just before take-off that they were not coming back as they were going to fly to Sweden, there to be interned for the duration. Another, uglier, rumour was swirling around the barrack blocks. This was that the Mackenzie crew had forcibly added the RAF police sergeant to their manifest, apparently with the object of disposing of him somewhere over the Baltic. Happily this particular rumour was seen to be without foundation when the sergeant returned from leave some days later. In the event, no communication was received from the aircraft after take-off and it was eventually posted as missing. Up to the time we left the squadron six months later there had been no further news so it looked as if the crew did not reach their Swedish haven, if that, indeed, was their intention.

This, then, was the backdrop to our Baltic trip on 28th April. We were to fly at ten thousand feet to the north of Denmark, turn south over the Kattegat, pass over Seeland west of Copenhagen, decending all the while until we reached our operational height of one thousand feet over the Baltic. As soon as we had made a positive identification of a coastal feature we were to set course for Lubeck, there to lay mines in the bay. We were warned to keep well clear of the German coast as the port was known to be heavily defended by searchlights and anti-aircraft. As Burma and I discussed the flight plan after briefing, it seemed to us that we had been given a near-impossible assignment. Burma appeared to be confident that he could navigate the aircraft to the target area. He was still smarting from the criticism directed at him after the Frankfurt trip and he was determined to show the rest of the crew that they could rely on him. However, the idea of flying, alone, at a thousand feet over the Baltic trying to find a landmark on which to fix our position was not an attractive one. I tried hard to think of a reason why we had been chosen for this most difficult mission. I know that I had upset the Squadron Commander by risking my aircraft and crew by pressing on to Frankfurt after losing an engine, but I did not think for a moment that there was any connection. Freddie was not that sort of person. In the end, I decided that it was no more than the luck of the draw and it was up to us to make the best of it. As we made our way to Met Briefing about two hours before take-off, Burma and I decided to keep our misgivings to ourselves. Our good intentions took a knock when we heard the Met Officer's forecast. Apparently a deep depression, building up over the eastern Baltic, was moving in a westerly direction and might affect visibility in the Lubeck area.

In wartime, the altimeter is the most important instrument on the pilot's panel. It works on barometric pressure and the pilot ensures that it is set to zero before take-off. As the aircraft climbs, the altimeter shows the height above the home airfield or base and as long as the aircraft returns to base there is no problem. However, should the aircraft be diverted to another airfield, particularly at night or in poor visibility, the ground level pressure at that airfield must be fed into the altimeter. This procedure, known as QFE, is standard practice for every pilot. The Met Officer had given us his estimate of the pressure in the Lubeck area, so that we could adjust our altimeter on arrival, but warned us that the pressure could drop still further if the depression was moving more rapidly than he had forecast. This would mean that we would be flying at a lower height than that shown on our altimeter, a situation fraught with danger on a low-level operation.

We flew eastwards in the darkness across the North Sea and made a visual identification of our turning point, the northern tip of Jutland. This was a good start and cheered us up considerably, especially Burma. Turning onto a heading of 160 degrees we flew over the Kattegat, losing height on the way. Flying over Seeland at two thousand feet the visibility started to deteriorate and I had difficulty in determining whether we were over land or water. Just about the time we were due to leave Denmark and reach the Baltic the whole situation changed. We became enveloped in thick unbroken cloud with visibility down to zero. After another ten minutes of hoping in vain for the cloud to lift, I realised that if I could not get below the cloudbase the operation would have to be abandoned. I decended slowly: 1500feet, 1000feet, still no break. 800, 600, 500. I heard an inner voice that was becoming more strident by the second. "Steady now, this is crazy." 300, 200 - still nothing. Then the inner voice became more insistent: "Your QFE is wrong. For God's sake, you'll hit the water."

"Captain speaking. I can't find the cloudbase so we're going home. Navigator, give me a course for the Kattegat." I was climbing as I spoke and levelled out at 2000 feet. Now the cloud was our protector, minutes earlier it could have been our destroyer. Shortly after Burma told me that, by his reckoning, we should be clear of Seeland and over the water, we came out of the cloud quite suddenly and I was horrified to see the moon shining out of a clear sky. Not quite a full moon but full enough to make us feel naked and vulnerable. Surely the Met Officer had got this wrong as well; this was not at all what we had been expecting. I was in no doubt what I had to do - get out as quickly as possible, as low as possible.

I went down to sea level and levelled off at 100 feet. The wind had ruffled up 'white horses' on the surface below; these enabled me to maintain height without reference to my instruments. The coast came up unexpectedly; before I knew it, I was looking at the Danish countryside flashing past below. I thought of Guy Gibson a few weeks earlier when he asked me if I thought I could handle low-level flying at night. Little did I think then that I would have an opportunity to test myself so soon. Apart from the apprehension, which was acute, I found our passage across Denmark most exhilarating, particularly when we flew up the main street of a sizeable town where, even at that late hour, people in the street waved to us as we roared past. Burma told me that the town was Viborg and that we were about halfway to the west coast and the comparative safety of the North Sea. The moon was shining more brightly now. Although we could be more easily seen, I could also see more clearly and this enabled me to fly closer to the ground. We had been told during training that at this height we could not be detected by enemy radar. Another advantage was that we could not be subjected to fighter attack from below, thus reducing the area of search for our gunners. Thankfully we reached the coast without incident and as I climbed to a more comfortable height I realised that I was drenched in sweat. Certainly low-level flying at night called for the ultimate concentration.

After six hours and forty-five minutes we landed back at Scampton with our mines still in the bomb bay. I was worried that the night's ordeal would not count towards our tour so I tackled the Flight Commander after de-briefing. "Sir, I know we brought our mines back, but this wasn't our fault. The Met forecast was all wrong. I hope the trip will count." John Leland smiled. "You can relax, it will count. I'll see to that." He was as good as his word.

Author's note:
At the time, I was delighted that, although we brought back our mines, our Baltic adventure would count as a completed

operation. I now realise that this was in accordance with the policy laid down by the Commander-in-Chief. In 'Bomber Harris, His Life and Times', Henry Probert writes, 'If the mines were brought back, he (Harris) explained to Portal (Chief of the Air Staff), it was because the Admiralty rightly insisted that they be laid accurately or not at all. The weather, therefore, was all-important but all too often very hard if not impossible to predict'.

Chapter 6

A Sitting Duck

As a result of the 'blow-up' on 15th March we lost so many aircraft destroyed or damaged that the squadron temporarily ceased to be operational. Other squadrons in the Group were ordered to hand over their surplus aircraft to 57 and, of course, took the opportunity of unloading their rogues and mavericks. 'J' - Jig was one of these aircraft, an old Mark One 'W' Series - W4946 to be precise - and I was far from impressed when I flew her on air test on the morning of 4th May. She was sluggish on the controls and there was a huge mag drop on one of the engines.

Although 'Chiefy' and his ground crew soon rectified the mag drop, I became more and more apprehensive throughout the afternoon about the coming night's operation. The target was to be Dortmund; we were in the middle of that phase in the Bomber Offensive that became known as the Battle of the Ruhr. German defences would be at their most effective - only Berlin provided sterner opposition - so it was essential that we could obtain maximum performance from our aircraft and I was not sure that 'J' - Jig could deliver.

We were half-way across the North Sea when my worst fears were confirmed. Try as I might, I could not coax or cajole 'J' - Jig above eighteen thousand feet. This was two thousand feet below the main Lancaster 'stream', leaving us more vunerable to night-fighters approaching from below. To make matters worse, Jig was losing altitude in the 'corkscrew' manoeuvres and I had to make good that height loss from time to time by opening the throttles and climbing. The exhausts on the Lancaster's Merlin engines always gave out a dull red glow at night. When the throttles were opened above normal cruising they became red-hot and must have been clearly visible to any fighter in the vicinity.

I had just completed my final climb to bombing height before making my run-in to the target when the aircraft was hit. It shuddered violently for several seconds and I saw smallish explosions in front of and slightly ahead of the aircraft. Almost immediately we were hit again, this time more violently, and I could see the same explosions ahead. When I heard the bullets ripping through the aircraft, the penny finally dropped and I shouted, "Rear gunner. It's a fighter. Can you see him?" There was no reply. Before I could take any evasive action we were subjected to a third attack. The control column slammed back into my stomach and Jig, heavily laden with her bomb load, pointed her nose skywards. As I could not push the control column forward the result was inevitable: the aircraft stalled and we seemed to be sliding sideways with the flames of Dortmund visible past the Engineer's head.

I closed all the throttles and with a despairing effort managed to push the control column far enough forward to enable me to wedge both my knees between it and my seat. My recollections of what followed are hazy and disjointed. We had taken three long bursts from a night fighter and we were falling out of the sky with a full load of bombs still aboard, not only out of control but also apparently uncontrollable. I can remember most clearly, first of all, the fear - a feeling which started in my stomach and went through my whole body and, secondly, the excruciating pain in my legs, pinned between the control column and the sharp metal edge of the pilot's seat. Although I did not realise it at the time, it was the position of my knees that saved us. Had they not been forcing the control column forward into a central position the aircraft would never have recovered and we would have carried on downwards until we hit the ground.

Fortunately, the aircraft was not spinning so I was able to replace my hands on the controls and try to ease the pressure on my knees, at the same time helping the aircraft's recovery. Gradually - and ever so slowly - the nose came up and we were straight and level. Our troubles, however, were far from over.

As I opened the throttles the pressure on my legs increased and with it the pain. I throttled back and shouted into the microphone: "Taffy I'm having difficulty with the controls. Stand behind my seat and help me push the column forward." This was the first time anyone had spoken since I had tried to contact the rear gunner but the bomb-aimer didn't even reply. He was behind my seat within seconds and was soon relieving the pressure on my legs. At the same time, the nose of the aircraft came down below the horizon and the airspeed increased. So far, so good. When the ailerons responded, albeit spasmodically, I felt as if I was regaining control.

My next action was to open the bomb doors and pull the jettison toggle. The loss of our bombs resulted in a significant easing of pressure on my legs although I still needed help from the bomb-aimer standing behind me. "Engineer from Skipper. Let me have a damage report." "Skipper from Engineer. All engines working OK, gauges normal. No sign of fuel loss." "Thanks, Stan. Stand by to take over from Taffy when he gets tired. I must have help." Stan's thumbs-up signal was clearly visible against the Dortmund fires. "Navigator from Skipper. Let me have a course for the return leg. I'm just turning onto a due north heading." "Navigator to Skipper. Keep on with 360 degrees. I'll try to obtain a fix on GEE and give you a correction." "Mid-upper here, Skip. I'm by the rest bed. The bastard shot off my jack plug. I'm going back to my turret but I will be out of contact." "Thanks Chris. Skipper to Wireless Op. Are you still with us?" "Joe here, Skip. What the hell is happening? My flimsies[1] are everywhere. Are we OK?" "Hope so, Joe. Now, Rear gunner let's hear from you." I waited a few seconds. "Rear gunner from Skipper. Can you hear me?"Ace Clark's voice sounded weak and distant: "Ace here, Skip. I think I've stopped something. Got a hell of a pain in my guts

1   'Flimsies' contained codes and colours of the day.
     They were printed on rice paper so that they could
     be swallowed by the wireless operator in the event
     of a forced landing on enemy territory

and my left arm won't work." "Do you need help?" "Not yet I don't. I've got one good arm and my turret still works." "OK Ace. Good man."

It was Stan's arm that helped me keep the control column forward and we had recovered most of the height that we had lost after the fighter attack. We had overshot our turning point by several minutes but Burma soon came up with a new course based on what he said was a very good fix. We were holding our altitude and making good airspeed although the aircraft must have suffered major damage. I already knew about the damage to the aileron and elevator contols, particularly the latter. On the other hand, the engines were behaving perfectly and the fuel supply seemed to be unaffected. After three sustained fighter attacks, we could scarcely believe our luck.

With a wounded rear gunner and a mid-upper out of contact in his turret we had little chance of surviving another attack, but no attack came. We had not heard from Ace for some time but eventually Chris's voice came over the intercom: "Mid-upper here, Skip. The bugger's shot off the heel of one of my flying boots as well." "Have you been hit?" My voice sounded anxious. "No, I don't think so. I've been back to the rear turret. The doors are all twisted but I prised them open with the axe. I pulled Ace out of the turret and dragged him to the rest bed." "How is he, Chris?" "Not good. I've given him a shot of morphine." "Thanks, Chris. Now get back to your turret as fast as you can."

Eventually we reached the North Sea and I put my mind to yet another problem: how to land the aircraft with virtually no control of its fore and aft movement and with unknown damage that could well make a safe landing impossible. I throttled back and pressed the undercarriage lever. Nothing happened. This was not unexpected and I still had the emergency system. At least, I hoped so. The outlook took a turn for the worse when I lowered the flaps; the pressure on the control column increased dangerously.

By the time we had reached the Lincolnshire coast I had made my decision. "Captain to crew. We are almost home but there is no way I can land the aircraft. When we get over base you are to bale out - so check your parachutes. Chris, you push Ace out of the door first, so check his harness, clip on his pack, and see that the ripcord is fixed to the static line." "Chris here Skip. If we do that we'll kill him. He's too badly wounded. There's a lot of blood and it looks as if he's caught a packet in his stomach." I did not reply. There was no point. Ace was one of us and - somehow - we had to find another way.

Over the North Sea, when I had time to take stock, I noticed that the wheel at my right hand which should have been operating the elevator trim was spinning around freely. The cable had apparently been severed in the last attack and this could be the cause of our problems. I pointed this out to Stan and he picked up a torch and went towards the back of the aircraft. A few minutes later his voice came through the intercom. "Stan here, Skip. I've found the end of the broken cable. I don't know what will happen if I pull it but I think it's worth a try." "Go ahead, Stan. I'll tell you're to stop if you're making things worse." Ever so slowly, the pressure came off my aching legs. "Keep going, Stan." I could not keep the excitement out of my voice. I pushed Taffy's hand off the controls and wached with unrestrained joy as the control column moved forward and remained there without assistance. "You've done it , Stan." I shouted. "Now fasten the cable to something so that it can't slip back again." At least we had a chance of getting the aircraft down in-one piece.

The lights of Scampton looked very welcoming after what we had been through but there was still danger ahead. I had no idea how the aircraft would behave when I tried to land. "Mayday, Mayday. Heron from 'J'- Jig. Request permission to land soonest. We have wounded on board. Wounded on board." We were cleared for landing and as we turned onto the down wind leg I asked Stan to operate the emergency system for the under-carriage. My heart leapt when I saw two green lights shining brightly on the panel. As I reached the funnel[2] I lowered the flaps, slowly at first, and then, as everything seemed in order, I pushed the lever all the way down. I took comfort from the thought of the many vehicles already rushing across the airfield in response to our Mayday call.

In the event, Jig behaved impeccably over what was to be the last few minutes of her flying life. The landing was a bit rough but the undercarriage held up and the brakes worked. We were soon following the Flying Control van into the dispersal nearest to the runway's end. As I cut the engines, I noticed the vehicles around the dispersal and people running towards the aircraft.

I was glad to have a helping hand down the aircraft ladder; my knees were hurting like hell. I hobbled clear of the dispersal. Someone stuck a cigarette in my mouth and lit it. Then I heard a scream and I realised I had forgotten all about Ace. As I reached the door Ace screamed again. Some medical orderly was attempting to pull him out of the door by his feet. Burma pushed the orderly away and hit him quite hard. Chris and Taffy slowly lifted Ace out of the aircraft and placed him on a waiting stretcher. I went with Ace to sick quarters. He had a broken arm and a very bad stomach wound. The Duty Medical Officer gave him first aid and he was soon on his way to the nearest RAF hospital. I had lost all the skin from my knees and was told to expect some nasty bruises but nothing was broken. I soon joined the rest of the crew at de-briefing. The briefing room seemed full of reporters who refused to let us go to bed until we had gone through every detail. The next day our brush with the night fighter and our uncomfortable journey home received extensive coverage in the national press. Even my parents were able to read about it in the Irish papers.

2   A funnel-shaped pattern of lights that indicated the correct approach to the flarepath.

In the morning I went to sick quarters to have my knees dressed and freshly bandaged. While I was there someone phoned Rauceby Hospital and found out that Ace was back from the operating theatre and out of danger. But his injuries were serious enough to ensure that the man from Moose Jaw would now be sent home.

After leaving sick quarters, I went with Joe and Stan to look at 'J'-Jig. She stood where we had left her the previous night. Even the spots of blood beneath the door were still there. The bomb bay seemed to have taken the main thrust of the attack. The bomb doors were scarred and twisted; one could only wonder why the bombs we were carrying had not exploded. Nine of the twelve propellor blades had bullet holes and one of the young airmen gleefully announced that he had counted 72 bullet holes in the aircraft. Several of these were visible in the rear turret. Clearly, Ace had been facing towards the port beam; he was 'side-on' to our attacker and this had almost certainly saved his life. The Engineer Officer, who had already carried out his examination, told me that Jig was now Cat.E - a complete write-off - and she would fly no more. The Armament Officer was also present. He said he found it hard to believe that the bomb load had not gone up and suggested that the explosions I had seen in front of the aircraft during the attack were from self-destroying ammunition which exploded at a predetermined range to help the fighter pilot judge the distance from his target.

Joe came out of the dispersal hut casually tossing a spent bullet in his hand. It had been presented to him by our wireless maintenance mechanic who had dug it out of the radio transmitter. The bullet had also penetrated the small hydraulic oil tank situated behind Joe's seat and the leaking oil had saturated his two homing pigeons, 'Smokem' and 'Pokem'. Sadly, they did not survive. All bomber crews took homing pigeons with them. If the aircraft came down in the sea - and the 'ditching' went according to the book - the wireless operator would attach a note showing the aircraft's position to each pigeon's leg in the hope that at least one of the pair would reach its home loft. Joe had become quite attached to 'Smokem' and 'Pokem'. Their names had been painted on their container and they flew with no one else. He was given a new pair of pigeons for our next and subsequent trips but the relationship was never quite the same.

My next visit was to the squadron commander's office, at his request, to talk through the previous night's attack and to hear my explanation of an incident that had lead to a complaint from the Station Medical Officer about an assault on one of his orderlies. I told him I would have done the same had I been near enough. We heard no more about it.

That afternoon I was summoned to 5 Group Headquaters to appear before the AOC, Air Vice-Marshal The Honourable Sir Ralph Cochrane. Apparently I was due to have a commissioning interview and the AOC gave instructions that it be brought forward so that he could talk to me about the previous night's attack. I told him I thought I got into trouble because I was in a sub-standard aircraft. He did not appear very sympathetic and said, "Someone has to fly them." However, after a 'Well done' he said that he was putting me forward for a commission.

Three days later, Chris, Taffy, Burma and I went to Rauceby Hospital to see Ace. He was propped up in bed with a wide grin on his face. As we came in he pointed to an ashtray on a table beside his bed, in which were two bullets. "Battle souvenirs," he said. "At least it's something to take home to Canada." "You're so lucky," said Burma. "If it hadn't been for the long-haired public schoolboy you wouldn't be here." "I know," said Ace, as he held out his good arm. Chris's handclasp was firm and the look on both their faces showed that all the animosity had gone.

Chapter 7

No Sympathy

The first time I saw Lal she was sitting alone in the saloon bar of the Saracen's Head in Lincoln. To say that she made an immediate impression would be an understatement. I had just been reading one of Raymond Chandler's novels and several of his descriptions of alluring females came to mind. She was not young - between 30 and 35 at a guess - slim, well-dressed, with her long hair tastefully arranged around her coat collar. Perhaps she wore a little too much make-up though she was surely out of my league. The fact that my smile brought no response was all the confirmation I needed.

I knew her name was Lal because Mary the barmaid had told me and one night after Lal had made another stunning appearance a couple of gin and tonics had Mary talking more freely than usual. Lal never came into the Saracen's Head, or left, with a man. Sometimes she was with a girlfriend but mostly she was alone. There was a strong rumour that she was married to a Royal Air Force officer who had gone missing in North Africa but Lal wouldn't answer any questions about her personal life. I was quite confident that I could have gleaned a bit more from Mary but, quite suddenly, she disappeared. I remembered that some weeks previously, when we had been enjoying a 'stand-down' in the Saracen's Head and listening to the bombers taking off, Mary had been quite specific about the target to be attacked. We dismissed it at the time as idle talk, but next morning we were horrified to discover that she had been right. Apparently someone else had overheard and contacted the security services. We never saw Mary again.

I did see Lal again, however. I was encouraged one evening by her answering smile but she refused my invitation to dinner. She said she might have a drink some other night but not now. I suppose I became obsessed with Lal and my visits to the

Saracen's Head became more or less routine. I had almost given up when it happened. She opened her handbag, took out an old envelope and wrote a telephone number on the flap. "Take this," she said. "When you next come back from operations, ring me up and I'll tell you where to come. I can offer you silk sheets and a good breakfast." "Why do I have to wait?" I said. "What if I don't come back?" "You'll come back," said Lal.

I took delivery of my new aircraft, ED944, on the morning of 12th May. It behaved well on air tests. Taffy levelled the bomb sight and the ground crew added a large 'I' to the squadron letters 'DX' already on the fuselage. The target that night was Duisburg. Joe, our wireless operator and Stan, our engineer, were not fit so we had Pilot Officer Stevens, an Australian, and Sergeant Dowding in their places.

Ruhr defences were the very best the Germans could devise. Most effective were the night-fighters working in conjunction with the searchlights. A master beam would, first of all, acquire an aircraft by radar. Once acquired, all the searchlights in the area would concentrate on, or 'cone', the poor unfortunate - the moth caught by millions of candlepower. Experienced pilots would wait until the searchlights had found a victim and then fly around the cone into the target area. There was nothing immoral about this. Everyone knew that some night it could well be their turn. Usually there was no escape for the trapped aircraft. Circling fighters were only too eager to queue up for the kill.

We had just started our bombing run when the cockpit was lit up by a vivid blue light - a light that grew in intensity by the second. I looked towards the ground and the dozens of pinpricks of light told me that tonight it was our turn. We had been coned. Tonight we were the victims and others could pass safely by. I had talked with other pilots who had escaped from searchlight cones and I had a rough idea of what I must do. Taffy, the bomb aimer, kept repeating, "I can't see anything,

Skip." I said, "Forget it" as I pulled the jettison toggle. Our bombs would fall short but the extra seconds could well be vital. As I closed the bomb doors I pushed the control column forward. We went from twenty to sixteen thousand feet in a matter of seconds and I noticed the airspeed indicator reading 350 mph. Then I pulled the column back and watched the airspeed fall off. When the aircraft started to judder I cut all four throttles, banked steeply and kicked hard on the top rudder. We fell like a stone into the darkness below. Slowly I opened the throttles and brought the aircraft back to a normal flying attitude. I glanced above me at the probing searchlights frantically looking for the moth that this time had managed to escape.

After we had cleared the target, I thought it wise to send Taffy down the fuselage to see if our escape had caused any damage. "Taff here, Skip. The contents of the Elsan are all over the place and I can't get past the ammunition belts. I doubt if our guns will work." Taffy was right. The gunners tested their guns over the North Sea and all of them jammed after only a few rounds. Thankfully, we hadn't needed them.

The manoeuvres over the target had taken a lot out of me. I really wanted to go to bed and sleep but I knew I had to ring Lal and call her bluff for in my heart I believed she would find another excuse. Imagine my surprise when she answered the telephone, gave me directions to her flat, and promised me a cup of tea on arrival. The WAAF driver on the flight van had a soft spot for me and I had no trouble in persuading her to take me out to dispersal. Before leaving I had given Lal's telephone number to Taffy, to be used only in dire emergency. My old Enfield motor-cycle was in its usual place in one of the bomb shelters. After checking that it had plenty of fuel I was soon out through the gap in the fence and on my way to Lincoln.

I was determined to find out why Lal shunned male companionship but it was nothing like as difficult as I imagined it would be. With a faraway look in her eyes she talked - and I listened. Her husband, a pilot with the Desert Air Force, had not returned from an attack on a German convoy. There had been no news and she said that she had felt for some time that she would not see him again. What made things more difficult was that on the night before she received the Air Ministry's telegram, her husband's parents had seen her having dinner with another man. The news had greatly affected her mother-in-law. She accused Lal of infidelity and called the telegram her punishment. Lal vowed that until she had some definite news about her husband, she would never appear in public with a man. She certainly kept her promise to me . The sheets were real silk and she gave me a marvellous breakfast, even though she served it around four o'clock in the morning. I asked her how many other men she had similarly entertained and she assured me that I was the only one. I was not inclined to believe her at first but as our loving went on through the night I found it easier to accept that she was telling the truth. Lal was one of the most beautiful women I had ever seen, she was shapely and passionate, and all the time I kept asking myself why on earth had she asked me to come to her flat just after I had returned from a raid on Germany. Then I recalled reading somewhere about primitive tribal women who obtained maximum sexual pleasure by seeking out the warrior who had just despatched his adversary in battle. And I had come directly from a battlefield ....

Then the telephone rang. "Taff here, Skip. For God's sake get back here as quick as you can. We're on tonight. Briefing is at fourteen hundred hours. Stan and Joe are still not fit but we've been given replacements. Paul Hawkins' engineer, Sergeant Bamlett is still standing in for Stan. He tells me it's full tanks." On the way back to Scampton I knew that there was no way I could fly on operations that night. I had had a rough time over Duisburg and since then I had made a lot of love to a very passionate woman and I had had no sleep whatsoever. The full tanks seem to point to another tough trip to Berlin and the crew I would be taking with me was an unknown quantity. Sergeant Todd, who had replaced 'Ace' in the rear turret, had flown with us for the first time last night and now we were to have two other strangers. Burma, Taffy, Chris and I held a council of war. They were sympathetic but also realistic. "You can't back out," said Burma "If the CO finds out that you were off the station last night, you'll be court martialled for sure. Have a cold shower and some black coffee and see how you feel." "Backing out won't help us," said Taffy. "They'll put in a sprog[1] pilot and then we really will be in trouble." It was no more than a minor compensation that the target was not Berlin. We were going to Pilsen in Czechoslovakia to attack the Skoda Works. There was a moment of hope when Chiefy told me that ED944 would not be ready. We had made a proper job of the ammo belts and it was taking the armourers a long time to sort them out. That hope was dashed when he told me that we were to take 'C'-Charlie. After that I discarded any idea of feigning illness or injury. Besides, I still felt I could fly a Lancaster.

The outward trip to Pilsen passed without incident. The defences around the target markers were negligible. This was not surprising as we were told later that the whole attack had been directed at a lunatic asylum in a small village some five or six miles from the Skoda Works. My lack of sleep seemed to have no effect on my skill as a pilot when we were over enemy territory. The urge for survival overcame the tiredness. But once we crossed the coast and reached the relative safety of the North Sea it was a different situation. The instruments on the panel in front of me seemed to change positions constantly, my head drooped forward and I lapsed from time to time into semi-consciousness. Taffy was told to stand behind my seat and to slap my face whenever my head went forward. The instruments kept changing position. Once the whole cockpit

1   'Sprog' is RAF slang for a novice

appeared to rotate through 360 degrees although I knew that the aircraft remained straight and level. I could not engage the automatic pilot as it was only the need for constant corrections to course and flying attitude that kept me conscious. I drifted off several times before we reached base as Taffy's slaps got harder and more frequent. "Come on, you're the only one who can fly this aircraft. Don't let us down now." A final super-human effort with the engineer double-checking the landing procedures and we were on the ground after seven hours and twenty five minutes.

My favourite was on the flight van and she took me to my sleeping quarters. I had sent a message to the Intelligence Officer that I was unwell and would see him in the morning. Burma told me he took off my flying gear. I don't remember that but I do vaguely recall people asking from time to time how I was. When I finally came to, Burma reckoned I had slept for twenty hours. I asked him what the new chaps had said about the previous night's performance. Burma said, "I told them that there was something wrong with your oxygen supply."

I only saw Lal once more. All she said was "Wasn't it fun?" I was going to ask her for a date but I had second thoughts. After all, I might have had to fly on operations on the following night.

Chapter 8

A Royal Summer

Apres Moi Le Deluge[1]

When we awoke on the morning of 17th May, we looked towards the nearby dispersal area being used for the aircraft of 617 Squadron. The empty spaces told us that a terrible price had been paid by those who had carried out the attack on the Dams. There was much sadness in the Sergeants' Mess but as they listened to the frequent radio reports triumphantly announcing the success of the raid, there was also much satisfaction. Previously, there had been some banter from the 57 crews when they returned from a rough trip to Germany and found the 617 crews relaxing after yet another training exercise. Now it was a different situation; there was nothing but admiration for those who had taken part in such a successful attack. There were countless stories to be told; one of the best came from 'Paddy' Hughes who had transferred from 57 Squadron with Geoff Rice. They lost their weapon on the outward journey when they flew too low and hit the water. 'Paddy' told anyone who would listen how the water rushed through the fuselage of his Lancaster and 'nearly drowned' him in the rear turret. Happily, he survived many more operations for I met him at a Pathfinders' Dinner after the war.

We thought that 'Butch' Harris might put in an appearance at Scampton after the raid. He was a distant commander, almost a mythical figure, who seldom visited his front-line squadrons, but the Dams Raid had been something special. My cockney wireless operator was convinced that 'the Butcha' was going to show up when the station's two squadrons were ordered to parade in 'best blue', in crews - pilots in front, by the Control Tower. When we lined up there was much speculation as to

1   Motto of 617 Squadron: 'After me, the flood'

who might appear, but none of us could really believe what was happening when a large limousine drew up beside Guy Gibson and out stepped the King and Queen. Naturally, the 617 crews got the star treatment but afterwards it was the turn of the 57 pilots. The King asked me how many trips I had done and wished me luck. The Queen just smiled and wished me luck as she held my hand, but that was enough. This most gracious of ladies had given me a tremendous lift.

We did not have to wait long for a visit from the Commander-in-Chief. We had just been 'stood down' for the day and were getting ready to take Lincoln by storm when the Tannoy crackled and ordered all 57 Squadron pilots to attend Station Headquarters for briefing at 15:00 hours. When we arrived at SHQ, two aircrew transports were already disgorging their loads. The silver wings worn with so much pride on the uniforms of the men jumping down from the vehicles identified them as the Poles from Hemswell and Ingham. No matter how quickly we cleared the target and made the return trip, we always found a Polish Wellington ahead of us. Those of us who had met the Poles soon discounted any idea that they might have come up short on their bombing runs.

The furniture in the briefing room was spartan in the extreme: tables, fold flat, and chairs, folding. As the minutes ticked by, the strumming of fingers on the table tops started to get on the nerves of even.those responsible. Suddenly, the whole room was brought to attention by the Station Warrant Officer. Through the door at the back came a posse of senior officers. Walking in front with the Commander-in-Chief was the Base Commander, Charles Whitworth. What a gem of a man the Air Commodore was; he knew the name of every pilot on his station, and of many of the other aircrew as well. Butch was smaller than I expected him to be. He walked with a slight stoop and his face had a greyish tinge as if he didn't spend enough time in the open air. I noticed Freddie Hopcroft, our own CO, and the AOC 5 Group - 'Cocky', the Honourable Sir

Royal visit.
RAF Scampton.

The King
standing under
the Squadron
Commander's
aircraft, 'F' -
Freddie

The King, accompanied by the Squadron Commander, Wing
Commander Hopcroft.

Ralph Cochrane, who had interviewed me for a commission just a few days previously.

The Base Commander introduced the C-in-C who spoke for about ten minutes. He told us that we should feel proud that we were the only fighting men who were able to hit back at the Hun and that we were hitting him mighty hard. He knew it was rough and all he could say was that it would get a lot rougher. He finished with these words: "I want you to look at the man on either side of you. In six months time only one of you three will be left, but if you are the lucky one, I promise you this: you will be two ranks higher."

After wishing us luck, the C-in-C strode towards the door, followed by his entourage. We immediately stood up and the men who had been strumming the table tops with their fingers started to hit them with the palms of their hands. The metal hinges on the tables made their own contribution to the clamour. When Butch was half-way to the door the Poles started to cheer. Everyone joined in and there seemed to be genuine affection for the man who had just told them that he would send them over Germany again and again until only one in three was left. One pilot was so carried away that he shouted out "Good old Butch." Charles Whitworth's stare warned him against any further indiscretions.

As the C-in-C reached the door he waved the other members of his party on and turned round to face his pilots. Suddenly, silence returned to the room. Butch half opened his mouth but no sound came. Instead he took a short step forward, lifted his arm in a smart salute, turned on his heel, and was gone[2].

2   My account of the Commander-in-Chief's address -
     and the reaction to it - has been summarized on pp
     199 - 200 of Henry Probert's Book, 'Bomber Harris
     - His Life and Times'. He uses this incident to
     illustrate the close bond that existed between the
     C-in-C and his aircrews.

Non-operational

When we reported for briefing on 29th May the route marked on the large map behind the platform looked familiar - we were going to 'Happy Valley' again. The target, however, was a new one: Wuppertal. Whereas at previous briefings the military importance of the target was always stressed, this time we were told that we were to drop our bombs on one of the Ruhr's dormitory areas. We were, in fact, going to burn the workers out of their homes and the numbers of these workers had increased significantly in the aftermath of the Dams Raid. Many had moved to Wuppertal when the floods had made their own houses uninhabitable. The policy of the 'area bombing' of German towns had been decided many months previously by our masters, but this was the first time that the policy had filtered down to the front-line squadrons.

We did not go to Wuppertal that night. While I was carrying out the full-throttle test on the port-inner engine in dispersal, I was subjected to the most excruciating pain in my left ear. A perforated eardrum was diagnosed and I was quickly transported to hospital. Local low-level flying was permitted after three weeks but I was not cleared for operations until we went to Cologne on 8th July.

The next six weeks were an unsettling time for the rest of the crew. They were likely to be called up at short notice to fill a vacancy in another crew, to replace someone who, for one reason or another, was not fit to fly on operations. To have to fly with the squadron commander or one of the flight commanders was just about acceptable but to fill a vacancy in a crew newly arrived on the squadron certainly was not. They were extremely lucky. Chris flew to Krefeld with Pilot Officer Hodgkinson on 21st June, but as far as I can remember, no one else was called upon.

The main enemy during this time was boredom. There were financial limits on the number of times one could go out dancing, drinking, or with a girl friend, in Lincoln. We spent several evenings each week in our quarters and we had to find our own amusement. Taffy, as might be expected of one who grew up in the Welsh valleys, had a fine baritone voice and his spirited rendition of such classics as 'The Volga Boatmen' and 'The Song of the Flea' were much in demand. Burma sat up until the early hours trying to solve the 'Times' crossword, smoking incessantly. When his cigarettes ran out, which was a regular occurrence, he went round the rest of us, even in the middle of the night, in his search for more supplies. Chris was so annoyed at these nocturnal interruptions that he left a packet of cigarettes at the foot of his bed and told Burma to help himself.

Another way of passing the time was to write comments in pencil against the operational trips recorded in the log books of other crew members. I made it quite clear that my pilot's log book was sacrosanct, but Chris's book contains several amusing entries. He had recorded - I am sure with some pride - that his well directed fire had discouraged three Ju88s from attacking us on our first trip to Berlin. Either Joe or Taffy had added 'Later identified as Wellingtons'. His entry for 4th May, which detailed our misadventures after our aircraft had been badly damaged by a fighter, was followed by the terse comment, 'Extra laundry charges three and sixpence'.

The first of these comments in Chris's log book is worth further examination. This related to our trip to St. Nazaire on 22nd March when we were 'fogged out' on our return and landed at Valley in the Isle of Anglesey with a 1000lb. bomb loose in our bomb bay. The pencilled comment was 'Stirling claimed as probable'. Shortly after leaving the target, Chris had reported that a Stirling had passed us at the same altitude and going in the opposite direction, and had fired at us in passing. At debriefing he added to his story by claiming that the Stirling's fire had come, not from its turrets, but from its fuselage. He was told in no uncertain terms by the Intelligence Officer that there were no Stirlings on the raid and, in any event, they couldn't get up to 19,000 feet. Chris immediately acquired the nickname of 'Stirling' Allen , a name that persisted some way through our tour. I would put forward two observations in Chris's defence. To start with, I saw the aircraft and I am quite sure that it was a Stirling. I noticed, first of all, four glowing rings coming towards me at considerable speed. As they came nearer I saw that they were the radial engines of a four-engined aircraft. As it flashed by, the high tail fin left me in no doubt that Chris's identification had been correct. I backed up Chris at briefing but my comments, too, were dismissed as the lunatic rantings of a new boy just out of training. I had suggested that the red-hot glow from the engines indicated that they were working at full boost, thus enabling the aircraft to reach a greater height than normal; the Intelligence Officer remained unimpressed. However, there were several reports later in our tour from crews who claimed that they had been attacked by four-engined 'battlewagons' which fired 'broadsides' at them as they passed. Reports of these attacks, which occurred during the period when the Germans marked the bomber stream with airborne flares, were treated with derision and disbelief. I have looked through post-war papers on the German defences for some mention of this method of attack, but in vain. It is just possible that it was tried out experimentally and then discounted as impractical. It was also possible that Chris had seen the first of these experimental 'battlewagons' over St. Nazaire.

During this period of operational inactivity my commission came through. I was given money to buy my uniform and told to report to the Officers' Mess in three days time. As I entered the mess bar it was full of officers having drinks before dinner. I looked around for someone who might talk to a lowly pilot officer. The 617 stars were there in force: Micky Martin, Joe McCarthy, Dave Shannon, all with their newly-won DSOs, but there was no sign of a friendly face from 57. I approached the bar and was waiting timidly for the barman to take my order when I heard a voice, "McCrea, how nice to see you here. What will you have to drink?" I turned my head and saw the Base

Commander, Air Commodore Whitworth, sitting at the end of the bar. He bought me a pint of bitter and introduced me as 'an old sweat from 57'. Charles Whitworth really knew how to make a new arrival feel at home.

I moved into what had been a married officer's quarter and shared a room with Brian Goodale, who had flown on the Dams Raid as Dave Shannon's wireless operator. 'Concave', as he was known, talked with some relish of the incident during a party in the mess when he tripped up and fell on the floor. Finding him motionless, his squadron colleagues assumed that he had succumbed to too much liquid refreshment. They laid him on his back on one of the mess tables and covered his body with a tablecloth that someone had taken from the dining room. The Station Chaplain was then brought down from his bedroom to conduct a 'burial service' over the 'corpse'. It was only when blood was noticed dripping from Concave's head that hilarity turned to concern, and the 'corpse' was quickly taken away for medical treatment. Brian Goodale talked little about the raid on the Dams. I know that he was greatly saddened by the loss of so many of his friends. He also said that it was unfair that the 617 crews were being lionised for one operation, no matter how spectacular or successful it had been, while the aircrews from other squadrons, risking their lives night after night, were receiving so little recognition. I did not agree. The Dams Raid had been received by the public with great acclaim. It had given a tremendous boost to the nation in general and to Bomber Command in particular. The journeymen aircrew of the main force were only too happy to bask in the reflected glory.

The Navigation Leader took advantage of our operational lay-off to send Burma, our navigator, on a refresher course. Ever since our three-engined sortie to Frankfurt in April, when we lost our way on the return journey, Burma's work had been under strict scrutiny. His log-work still didn't measure up so he was replaced by 'Jock' Glencross, thus adding another nationality to our crew.

Aircrew and Groundcrew
Lancaster ED944 'I' - Item.

Joe - Burma - Vic - Jock - Taffy - Chris
Bob - Paddy - Stan
Ron - Curly - Freddie - Jim - Tom

(Bob Sherrett was our tail gunner on all the Hamburg
raids).

July, 1943

Last cigarette

Chapter 9

The Battle of Hamburg

In the space of six days, from 24th to 29th July, 1943, Bomber Command despatched three 'maximum effort' raids of just under 800 aircraft against Hamburg; all these raids were highly successful. Three days later, more than 700 aircraft took off to bomb the city but almost half were unable to attack due to extremely severe and dangerous weather conditions over the target area. Flying in our regular aircraft, ED944, we took part in all four raids.

Hamburg had gained a reputation on 57 Squadron as a tough target. The squadron had not attacked the city since early March when the Commanding Officer, Freddie Hopcroft, was reputed to have had a rough passage. Thereafter, when briefing crews for raids on other German targets, he frequently tried to raise morale by telling them that the defences they were to face were nowhere near the standard of those protecting Hamburg. It was with some trepidation, therefore, that we prepared to attack Hamburg on 24th July. We took some comfort from the news that we were flying into battle with a brand new weapon - 'Window'. Window consisted of bundles of metallic strips which were ejected from each aircraft at sixty second intervals. If enough strips were thrown out in the same location, each 'swarm' would produce an echo on German radars similar to a bomber aircraft. It was hoped that these false echoes would so confuse the operators that they would be unable to control and direct the searchlights, flak and fighters protecting the city against attack.

In the event, this is exactly what happened. Searchlights either waved aimlessly through the sky or remained upright waiting for radar instructions that never came. Flak was spasmodic, the gunners having to make do with putting up barrages at random, and the radar- controlled fighters were unable to operate. Only twelve aircraft were lost out of a force of 792, the lowest loss rate ever on a major raid.

Under perfect flying conditions and against largely impotent defences, this first raid on Hamburg was the most straightforward and least dangerous that any bomber crew would ever experience. Our crew was no exception. Quite untroubled by the defences, we joined the apparently endless stream of bombers flying across the city and releasing their bombs into the fires below.

We flew back to base without incident, giving thanks for 'Window' which had ensured such a peaceful and uneventful trip. I remember the Squadron Commander's words at de-briefing "Enjoy it while you can. The Germans will soon find an answer. They will not leave you alone for long." The answer came much more quickly than anyone who flew over Hamburg on the early morning of 25th July would have thought possible.

We had been told at briefing that the raid on Hamburg would be the first in a series so it was something of a surprise when we were detailed to attack Essen on the following night. As far as we were concerned, however, a defective engine necessitated an early return. Although Bomber Command gave Hamburg some respite, the Americans did not. Making their first raids of the war against a heavily defended target, they launched daylight attacks on each of the two days following the first raid. Although they caused significant damage, their defensive box formations were not as efficient as they had hoped they would be and their losses were severe.

In hindsight, the second RAF raid on Hamburg on 27th/28th July, 1943, was a landmark for Bomber Command. The raid was the heaviest and most destructive ever mounted. My log book contains comment that 2400 tons of bombs were dropped in 45 minutes. 787 aircraft took off. Probably as many as 750 attacked the target and 17 failed to return. The raid was, with one exception, similar to the first. The searchlights were uncoordinated, flak erratic and apparently ineffective and we saw no fighters. The exception was the target itself. During the first raid we looked down on a number of conflagrations; several areas of the city were well alight and burning fiercely. During the second raid, the whole city was on fire. On our bombing run we seemed to be approaching an active volcano, which was continually exploding and erupting, and into which more bombers were dropping their high explosives and incendiaries. The heart of the volcano was glowing bright red and the column of smoke was already higher than the approaching bombers.

The image of the burning of Hamburg on the morning of 28th July, 1943, will remain with those who saw it for the rest of their lives. In the years to come there would be many reports of the 'firestorm' and the horror it brought to the citizens of Hamburg. These reports would cause much heart-searching and self-recrimination for many aircrew, but on the night in question we were only concerned with hitting the target and returning safely to base.

The fires were still burning when the bombers launched a third raid on the city some 48 hours later on the 29th July. Once again it was 'maximum effort': almost 800 aircraft and their crews were listed on the Battle Orders pinned up in the messes and crew rooms throughout Bomber Command. Crews were warned at briefing that it was more important than ever to stay in the bomber stream. 'Window' would give no protection to stragglers or those off track. All enemy night-fighters were expected to operate just outside the main stream of bombers, where radars would still be able to acquire their targets. Half of the 57 Squadron aircraft were to attack in the first two waves, immediately after the Pathfinders. These two waves were to drop their bombs at 'Z' plus 5 and 'Z' plus 10 minutes respectively. The remaining nine aircraft were assigned to the fifth wave of the attack, and their designated time-on-target caused some consternation. There was usually five minutes between waves so the fifth wave could have expected to bomb at 'Z' plus 25 minutes. Instead, the time-on-target was 20 minutes later at 'Z' plus 45. As we were one of the aircraft involved, I queried the timing. Briefing for this particular raid was being carried out by one of the flight commanders, who did not seem unduly concerned. It was only when another pilot also challenged the timing and suggested that Group Headquarters be asked to confirm, that the Briefing Officer responded. Some minutes later he returned to the briefing room and announced that the timings for the fifth wave of the attack stood.

We were almost an hour's flying from Hamburg when we first saw the fires. These grew in intensity as we approached and we could see the extensive flak barrage and hundreds of searchlights probing the night sky. Then, as we reached the outskirts of the city, everything stopped. Everything, that is, except the fires; although these were nothing like the 'active volcano' of the previous raid, they were still an awesome sight. There were a few flak bursts in the distance but none over the target. Not a single searchlight challenged our approach. I had been long enough on the squadron to pay heed to the old maxim: 'When the flak stops, look out for fighters', so I warned the gunners to be wide-awake. We didn't see any fighters over Hamburg - we didn't see any bombers either. It soon became clear that our target time had been wrong. The raid was over, everyone was on the way home. Everyone, that is, except for the poor unfortunates from 57 Squadron who were over the city on their own. Records show that of the 702 aircraft that dropped their bombs on the night of 29th/30th July, ED944 was the 701st. The journey across and above a blazing Hamburg was one of the strangest I have ever undertaken. No one fired at us, no fighter attacked us, no searchlight was pointed in our direction. But as I turned away after dropping our bombs, I have never felt so exposed and so vunerable. All I could do was to fix my eyes on the darkness beyond the fires and pray that we could reach that darkness before we were spotted by a fighter. Although we managed to fly clear without incident, one of our colleagues was not so lucky. I watched as a bomber just ahead and slightly below was subjected to a series of attacks from a fighter. It burst into flames and soon commenced its final fiery spiral into the earth below.

I felt very relieved when I landed back at Scampton later that morning. I also felt very angry. Of the nine aircraft held back in error, Flight Sergeants Parker and Allwright failed to return. I knew that I had watched one of these two crews being shot down but I did not know until many years later that it had been Allwright. At de-briefing the Intelligence Officer admitted that our target time had been a mistake. The error had been discovered shortly after we had taken off. We wondered, if this were so, why we had not been recalled. We also wondered if the officer in charge of last night's operation had ever bothered to query the time with Group Headquarters as he had been asked to do. It may be significant that the officer in question disappeared that night off the station and we never saw him again.

The fourth raid on Hamburg was despatched on 2nd August. The raid had been postponed for 24 hours due to a violent thunderstorm that had affected most of south and central England throughout the previous day and night. The meteorological experts had advised Bomber Command that the storm, which was rapidly moving eastwards, would be well clear of the Hamburg area before the bombers arrived. They were completely and utterly wrong, a mistake which would be directly responsible for the loss of many aircraft and their crews.

For our part, the outward journey was uneventful as we crossed the German coast near Heide and continued in the direction of Lubeck. As we approached the coast, there was evidence of much more fighter activity than we had seen on the previous raids. After reaching a point north of Hamburg the entire bomber stream turned to attack the city. It was at this point that our suspicions that the meteorologists had made a mistake were confirmed. The storm clouds that had been over England some 24 hours earlier were now dead ahead, dark and forbidding, and towering above the bombers by several thousand feet. I realised that what I first took to be flak were in reality lightning flashes emanating from the storm clouds that we were rapidly approaching. As we flew into the lightning-charged clouds the effect was immediate and terrifying. The air currents came first, throwing the aircraft from side to side as well as up and down. One could almost hear the airframe protest as it was subjected to these external forces. The lightning was continuous; as it flashed one could see that the clouds were sometimes broken up by eerie canyons and ravines. Blue electrical discharges flashed between the muzzles of the guns, and our propellers looked like catherine wheels, as if a torch had been fastened to the end of each blade. From time to time the whole aircraft became shrouded in a blue shimmering light. This was my first and only experience of St. Elmo's Fire, a phenomenon that mystified those who manned the sailing ships of the nineteenth century.

Worst of all was the icing, which was invisibly building up over the entire aircraft. The controls were becoming stiff and sluggish and the aircraft slow to respond. The propellers would periodically throw off particles of ice which could actually be heard striking the wing areas. We were flying into the dreaded cumulo-nimbus and into the worst electrical storm that anyone could ever imagine. To carry on in such conditions would be foolhardy so I told the crew that we were turning back. I jettisoned our bomb load and gradually and with some difficulty turned the aircraft on to a reciprocal heading. A badly shaken and silent crew were greatly relieved to escape from the terrors of nature and were happy to reach base without further incident.

The final raid on Hamburg was an expensive failure. Hundreds of bomb loads were either dropped or jettisoned in the open countryside or on small towns and villages surrounding Hamburg but only a few aircraft dropped their bombs on the city. Most crews had to endure the very real horrors of the electrical storm and many had difficulty in retaining control of their aircraft. Thirty-three aircraft in total failed to return. Research after the war showed that the loss of as many as ten of these may have been directly due to adverse weather conditions. One of the pilots forced, with his crew, to abandon his aircraft over the sea because of ice was my good friend from training in America, Alex McGarvey. Alex and his wounded navigator were the last to leave the stricken Stirling and, luckily, were able to link up in the darkness by using their aircrew whistles. Alex had been a Glasgow policeman and was an exceptional swimmer. He attempted to tow his navigator to the German coast but was eventually forced to give up. Having given his 'Mae West' (life jacket) to his wounded comrade, Alex set off by himself towards a distant light which turned out to be an anchored light vessel. He persuaded the German crew to rescue his navigator and both men spent the rest of the war as prisoners. On the strength of his navigator's report, sent through the Swiss Authorities, Alex was awarded the George Medal.

Authors Note:
Details of routes flown, together with aircraft numbers and losses, have been taken from Martin Middlebrook's book 'The Battle of Hamburg'. He also refers to the incorrect time-on-target given to the last-wave aircraft from 57 Squadron.
In an appendix, the 57 Squadron losses are listed as follows:
Lancaster ED616 (F/Sgt G.A.N. Parker), 25th down on 3rd raid by Hamburg flak. 7 killed. Crew on 7th operation.
Lancaster ED931 (F/Sgt. E.F. Allwright), 26th down on 3rd raid by fighter attack. 6 killed, 1 prisoner. Crew on 21st operation.
Lancaster JA696 (F/Sgt. A.C. Browning), 15th down on 4th raid, cause unknown. 7 killed. Crew on 1st operation.

After the Hamburg raids I felt that I had earned my leave. I had arranged with the Flight Commander that a new crew would fly to the North of Ireland on a training flight and drop me off. I flew JA896 'D'-Dog to the Royal Naval Air Station at Maydown, near Londonderry. It was supposed to be training for the new crew but I could not resist the opportunity of making a low-level approach to the Irish mainland. Anyway, I thought that Sergeant Fearn would have enough time for training on the return journey. I did not receive much of a welcome at Maydown. The Commanding Officer, a lieutenant commander, rode up on his bicycle and berated me for landing 'a dirty black bomber' on his precious airfield. I spent my leave at Portrush, with its wonderful beaches and splendid golf course, and tried to relax and forget, even if only for a few days, the slaughter that was taking place almost every night both on the ground and in the air.

When I arrived back at Scampton, I learned that 'D'-Dog, which had taken me on leave and so annoyed Maydown's commanding officer, had crashed on the airfield after returning from an attack on Milan. Flight Sergeant Smithers and his crew had joined the squadron the day before I had gone on leave and it was their first operation; five of the crew died in the crash. But the topic on everyone's lips was the raid on a place called Peenemünde on Germany's Baltic coast. No one was really sure what they had attacked. There had been talk at briefing about production of new radar equipment to be used against the bombers, but the Commanding Officer had been unusually vague. It was only when he read out a signal from the Commander-in-Chief that the aircrews realised that they were about to be involved in something very important. The signal stated that the target was so vital that if it was not destroyed at the first attempt the crews would have to go back, again and again, until it was.

The attack had been carried out from 8,000 feet under a full moon. Although successful diversionary tactics had kept the night-fighters clear of the target area until the early waves of bombers were on the way home, the later waves, made up of Lancasters from 5 Group, found a hostile reception awaiting them and suffered heavy losses. Out of 117 Lancasters despatched from 5 Group stations, 17 did not return, a loss rate of 14.5%. One of the casualties was 57 Squadron's new Commanding Officer, Wing Commander W.R. Haskill, DFC, flying in ED989, the aircraft that he had just taken over from Freddie Hopcroft. In total, 40 aircraft and their crews were lost. Although I was not involved, Peenemünde is worthy of mention as the only main force precision raid carried out by Bomber Command. The purpose of the raid did not become clear for some considerable time. Eventually it turned out that Peenemünde was Hitler's Rocket Research Establishment and although the damage may have been less than expected, it was sufficient to delay the deployment of the German V2 rockets for several months. The operation is covered in detail in Martin Middlebrook's splendid book ' The Peenemünde Raid, 17/18th August 1943'. The accounts of the numerous air battles, from both RAF and Luftwaffe viewpoints, make fascinating reading.

'Burma' -
newly
commissioned

John Kimber. Our
rear-gunner for six of
our last eight trips.

A well-known photograph taken at Scampton. The Lancaster in the foreground is 'W' - Willie, flown by a Dutchman. 'Dutchy' Haye claimed that if he was shot down over his native Holland he would be back in a week. He made good his boast.

Chapter 10

Changing Tactics

'But the most dramatic transformation of the bomber war in 1943 and 1944 was brought about by the decision of both sides to turn night into day.

....the most dazzling firework display in history now exploded every night over Germany. British Pathfinders dropped flares to light the target for their markers, while high above them the Luftwaffe aircraft were laying their own lines of parachute flares to illuminate the bombers for fighter attack'.

'Bomber Command'
Max Hastings

When I returned from leave in mid-August the squadron was preparing to move from our comfortable accommodation at Scampton to a new airfield at East Kirkby, almost half-way between Lincoln and the coast. This was to allow for the construction of concrete runways at Scampton. Up to this time we had to lift our heavily laden Lancasters off grass, as indeed had the 'Dambusters' when they left on their famous raid. East Kirkby was primitive and functional: ten officers sleeping in a hut, outside washing facilities, and a walk through the mud to the Mess, which itself was devoid of any comfort. Off duty the attention of the crews moved from Lincoln to Boston, where the 'Gliderdrome' dance hall gathered all the local talent under one roof. We packed our personal belongings in the back of ED944 and landed at East Kirkby on 29th August, 1943. Two days later we were one of 14 crews detailed to attack Berlin.

The previous CO had warned us that it would not take the Germans long to overcome the disruption to their defences caused by 'Window', used for the first time against Hamburg a month previously. He was right. Faced with the continued use of 'Window', the German scientists soon realised that they could no longer rely on ground-controlled fighters to provide the main defence against the British bombers. It was perhaps possible to vector fighters towards aircraft flying on the fringes of the bomber stream where their own airborne radar might still be effective but elsewhere in the stream they were largely blind and impotent. To meet the challenge, the Luftwaffe formed, with all possible speed, several squadrons of single-engined day-fighters, made up mainly of the Me 109s that were being deployed against the American box formations. These 'Wild Boar' squadrons, as they were known, were positioned on carefully selected airfields and 'scrambled' to intercept the bombers as they came within range. The great majority of these pilots had little experience of flying at night and there were many accidents. Once they had made contact with the bombers, however, the pilots felt much more at home. Bright flares had been dropped along both sides of the bomber stream, virtually turning night into day. No longer operating in the dark, the 'Wild Boar' pilots engaged the passing bombers with new-found enthusiasm and considerable success.

As we flew towards Berlin I watched with some trepidation as the new German defence system unfolded ahead. The flares on either side of the stream had turned the area between into a brightly lit arena in which dozens of bombers were clearly visible. Among them flew the fighters selecting suitable targets to attack. The route selected took the bombers towards Hannover - to encourage the Germans to prepare for an attack on that city - only to re-direct them at the last minute towards Berlin. We were in the first wave of the attack, bombing directly after the Pathfinders at 'Z' plus 5 minutes, yet the flares kept appearing on either side of our planned route at least fifteen minutes ahead of our position. Apparently the Germans were making an inspired guess at the route the bombers intended to take. This alarming fact was reported emphatically by the returning crews and there were even some suggestions that the possibility of a breach of security should be examined. On this particular raid, however, we encountered no trouble. The target was bombed successfully and we arrived back at East Kirkby after a round trip of seven hours and ten minutes.

Three days later we were again one of 14 of the squadron's aircraft detailed for another attack on Berlin. This trip was to be much more exciting. The bombers flew more or less the same route as before, again flying directly towards Hannover before turning towards Berlin. On either side of the route the flares burned at intervals, their attempts to lighten the darkness helped by the splendour of the 'aurora borealis' shining brightly off our port beam. For most of the route we were flying over ten-tenths cover; this meant that the bombers were silhouetted against the reflection of the flares in the clouds below. I watched as our change of course north of Hannover was clearly marked by flares several minutes ahead of the first bombers. There was neither flak nor searchlights; there was no need. The bombers were clearly visible across the entire width of the stream. On the other hand, although the fighters could see their targets, they were deprived of the advantage of approaching them under cover of darkness. All RAF gunners were opening up at much longer range, hoping to discourage the fighters from pressing home their attacks. We had been told at briefing that the pilots employed in this new defence system had little experience of night combat and returning crews were able to confirm that most were reluctant to continue an attack on an aircraft whose gunners were returning fire.

We had managed to avoid fighter attack until we had dropped our bombs and were turning away from the target area. Our rear-gunner for this trip was Sergeant Lamble, who had not flown with us before, but he proved his worth when his message came over the intercom: "Rear gunner here. Fighter approaching from starboard below. Prepare to corkscrew starboard. Corkscrew starboard .... Go." His timing was precise and as I dived to starboard I saw out of my window the fighter's tracer pass harmlessly by. "Well done, rear gunner.

Any sign of him?" "Can't see anything. Hold it ... Yes, there he is, coming in from the same angle. Prepare to corkscrew starboard. Steady.." I heard the comforting chatter of Lamble's 303s as I waited. "Starboard ... Go." He had called it right again and the tracer was further away. "Mid-upper here, Skip. I got in a good burst as well. I think he has had enough." "Very good, everyone, but keep your eyes open. Navigator, give me the return heading." "Right, Skip. It's 274."

As we pulled away from the fires of Berlin I was struck by the sudden lack of activity. No searchlights and no one shooting at us. Even the flares had disappeared. Because there were now no flares the 'aurora borealis' had taken on a new intensity. Even in our precarious situation I could not help but marvel at its beauty. And then the penny dropped. The 'aurora' was still on my side of the aircraft. We were flying east. Towards Russia. "Skipper to Navigator. We're in trouble. I've been flying a reciprocal. How long have I been doing it?" "Twelve minutes, Skipper." "Skipper to crew. I've made a mistake and we've been flying east. It's too late to try to make it home alone across Germany. We'll go north to the Baltic and land in Sweden if we have to. Give me a new heading, Navigator."

We flew alone and unmolested with the Northern Lights beckoning us towards the sanctuary of Sweden. After just under an hour we found ourselves over the bright lights of a neutral country and I switched on our navigation lights to convey to the inhabitants that we had no malicious intent. Our intrusion was soon noted. The rear gunner announced that an aircraft, displaying lights, was approaching fast from below and behind. The Swedish pilot positioned himself on our port wingtip and, after flashing his lights, turned his aircraft ninety degrees to port. He then flew for a few minutes slightly above and behind our aircraft before returning to our wing tip and repeating his turning manoeuvre. The message was clear; we were not welcome in Sweden. During the flight northwards the Navigator and Engineer had between them worked out that, if necessary, we should have just enough fuel to reach England. I decided to put their calculations to the test so after a friendly waggle of our wings I switched off our lights and turned westwards to fly across Denmark and the North Sea towards home.

We set our engines at maximum economy and commenced a shallow dive in order to maintain a reasonable speed over a country whose defences were an unknown quantity. In the event, our journey back to England was trouble free; our only concern was fuel. Jock Glencross, our navigator, was obtaining first-class fixes from his GEE and although we were flying north of our planned route he remained confident that we could make it. In order to cut some miles off our journey, I asked for a diversion to a Yorkshire airfield and was directed to land at RAF Topcliffe. We came straight in without formality.

Topcliffe was an all-Canadian bomber station and we were royally welcomed by the station commander himself, an Air Commodore, who pressed a large cigar on each member of the crew. After reporting our safe arrival, we were treated to the largest steaks any of us had seen in years and provided with the most sumptuous sleeping quarters. Not surprisingly, we gained the impression that Canadian aircrew were being looked after extremely well.

The next morning we took 200 gallons of fuel on board and set off for East Kirkby. As it was only a short journey, we did not climb to any great height. Indeed, I took the opportunity of getting away from the grind of bomber operations, and at the same time expressing my joy and relief at the previous night's safe return, by flying the aircraft at tree-top height for most of the journey. I did not realise until I had landed how near I came to ending the war for myself and all the crew.

As we neared East Kirkby I climbed to one thousand feet and obtained permission to land. On the downwind leg, the port-outer engine spluttered and stopped. Stan feathered the blades immediately. As we lined up on the runway, the propellers on the starboard-inner engine started to windmill as it failed as well. Luckily we were in a good landing position so I cut all the throttles and allowed the Lancaster to glide towards the runway. Over the boundary hedge the third engine stopped. The landing was perfect and as we ran along the runway there was a strange silence as the remaining engine ceased to function. Only then did Stan and I realise what had happened and we both pointed at the fuel cocks at the same time. We had taken on fuel at Topcliffe but neither of us had checked that the fuel cocks were set to draw fuel from the tanks that had received it. The flight van was alongside by the time we came to a stop in the middle of the runway. Thankfully, the first person out of the van was Flight Sergeant Booth. I quickly left the aircraft and taking him aside told him what had happened. I well knew even then that if the facts became known it would certainly mean a Board of Enquiry and possibly a Court Martial. All 'Chiefy' said was "We'll look after you, Sir." He was as good as his word. The aircraft had stopped on the runway due to suspected overheating. The ground staff had towed it away and now all engines were working perfectly. I called round later to thank him. He said, "I'm glad we were on the spot to sort out the problem."

As I looked back on this raid I could not help thinking that many aircrews that night had carried out their duties perfectly and yet they were now either dead or missing. I had made two cardinal errors and we had survived. The first mistake could happen to any pilot and has happened to most but the second mistake was unforgivable. As soon as a trainee pilot sits in his first cockpit he is taught that his 'vital actions' are absolutely essential to his survival. These actions are so important that he is given a mnemonic to commit to memory so that no action is ever missed out. He goes through them before starting up and again before taking off. Our journey from Topcliffe was, in my opinion, so unimportant and routine that I neglected to give it the attention it demanded and we almost paid a terrible price. Had our fuel run out a few minutes earlier our only hope would have been a crash landing in the open countryside. Many years later, someone remarked that I must be the only pilot who ever landed a Lancaster on one engine. Maybe I was, but it was an event in which I take no pride. On the credit side, I never forgot my 'vital actions' again.

Chapter 11

Search and Rescue

The villagers of East Kirkby extended their warm hands in friendship to the newly-arrived aircrew. But the 'Red Lion' was usually crowded and many airmen sought recreation in Boston, travelling there by whatever means possible. As a crew, we found the people of Boston extremely hospitable, particularly one or two families whose homes were always open if we wished to stay overnight. Nothing was too much trouble for them. On one occasion the family's fourteen year old daughter even gave up her room. We were told that she was going to spend the night with a friend a few doors away; next morning we discovered that she had spent the night on cushions beneath the kitchen table.

I had brought my motor-cycle from Scampton and I usually took a member of the crew on the pillion, meeting up with the others in the town. On this particular evening Chris was the passenger and we set out across the flat fen-land of East Lincolnshire, skirting the little villages where we might be stopped by the local policeman asking awkward questions about our petrol supply. The road was anything but straight. Its direction was determined by the many ditches or dykes which ran alongside. These abounded in a variety of sizes and shapes, all filled with water of unknown depth. We proceeded by way of a sequence of right-angled bends, not too difficult to negotiate in the daylight, but an entirely different matter in the dark as we were to find out to our discomfort some hours later.

I cannot remember what exactly we did in Boston. Possibly a brief visit to the local dance hall, the Gliderdrome, and possibly one or two drinks. Certainly no more, as we could be getting ready for operations within hours. But I do remember that Chris and I decided not to stay overnight and we set out on our return journey to East Kirkby long before the pubs and the dance hall had closed their doors. The night was dark and scattered patches of fog made it difficult to stay in contact with the road verge which was our only navigational aid. Most of the journey was behind us when in a particularly dense patch of fog I lost contact with the verge. I braked, but it was too late. The road had turned left but we had gone straight on. There was a bone-shaking bump as we hit the opposite side of the road, a few more yards over rough ground, and then beneath us there was nothing. Both of us - and the motor-cycle - were falling into oblivion.

My old Enfield hit the water first. I went over the handlebars and followed. The water was cold, it smelt foul and tasted even worse. As I broke the surface I pushed down with my feet and was thankful to touch the bottom. "Chris, where are you?" There was a touch of panic in my shout. "OK Skip, I'm right beside you." Chris's voice was as calm as ever. We struggled over to the edge of the ditch and pulled ourselves up the bank and on to the road. "What now?" said Chris. "We're a long way from the airfield and I'm cold." "We passed a house a few moments back," I said. "You must have noticed the poor blackout in the front room. Let's go back and see if they will help us to dry off."

We found the house quite easily, guided by the chink of light shining out below one of the curtains. The house was small, typical of the Lincolnshire countryside and probably occupied by a farm labourer and his family. The fact that there was a light in the front room gave us the courage to knock on the door. After a silent pause and a second knock the voice sounded gruff: "Who is there and what do you want?" "Two airmen from the airfield. We've had an accident on our motor-cycle. Could you help us please?" We heard the bolts being pulled back and the door was opened by a man holding a Tilley lamp towards us so that he could see us properly. The lamp had clearly come from the front room as the chink of light had disappeared. "You had better come in. Are you hurt?" His voice was softer now. "No, but we are very wet. We went into the ditch," said Chris. "If you could let us have a couple of old towels we could have a rub down." "Come in," said the man. "Let's see what we can do for you." By this time his wife had appeared. She produced mugs of steaming tea, buckets of hot water, towels and two large grey shirts which came down to our knees. After removing the mud from our bodies and our uniforms we accepted the couple's offer of an easy chair each for the night and were soon asleep.

The man's voice was insistent. "Come on, wake up. There's a lot of activity at the corner where you went into the ditch. RAF people and they seem excited. You had better go and show yourselves." Putting on our uniforms was difficult but we managed. My 'fore and aft' cap had been in my pocket and was almost dry. Chris had lost his; presumably it was in the ditch. After declining the couple's offer of a mug of tea, we thanked them both for their kindness and left.

As we walked towards the scene of the previous night's incident, we could see two RAF police vehicles and at least four service policemen, apparently under the control of a Flight Sergeant, who was directing operations. Two of the policemen were throwing out some kind of grapple and as we got nearer I could see that their target was the handlebar of my old Enfield which was protruding about twelve inches out of the water. Floating near it was Chris's cap. Chris had reached the Flight Sergeant. "We're all right, Flight. We're not hurt and the people in that house put us up for the night." The Flight Sergeant's face gradually took on a purple hue as he slowly looked Chris up and down. "Bloody hell. Here we are trawling for your body and you've been tucked up in bed." "Well not exactly, Flight, but we'll be glad if you can give us a lift back to the airfield." Before the Flight Sergeant could answer, I said, "The motor-cycle belongs to me, Flight. I'll look after it." The Flight Sergeant had not noticed me before and he spun round immediately. I looked no more presentable than Chris and I was subject to the same scrutiny. But as soon as the Flight Sergeant's eyes reached the pilot officer braid on my sleeve he

came to attention in a smart salute. "Glad you're all right, Sir."
"Yes I am, thank you. I'm sorry to have given you all this work,
but you can leave the motor-cycle to me. I'll get in touch with
our ground crew in 'A' Flight and I'm sure I can persuade them
to come and collect it."

Our flight crew did more than collect the cycle. They stripped
it down and cleaned it and re-assembled it piece by piece.
When the job was finished the old Enfield had never run so
sweetly. Next time Chris and I went to Boston, however, we
took the Liberty Coach. You could hardly blame us.

Chapter 12

Stop-Start
Towards The Finish

False Dawn

Three days after our infamous Berlin experience ending in a single-engined landing we went to Munich. Just before leaving Scampton we had flown to Nuremberg with John Kimber as rear gunner and he now joined us on a permanent basis - our sixth occupant of the rear turret. When I flew my 'second pilot' trip to Wilhelmshaven with Paul Hawkins in February, John Kimber had been with us as a regular member of Hawkins' crew. He had later been sent for training as a Gunnery Leader and during the time he had been away from the squadron Hawkins completed his tour . John returned to find himself without a crew and happily joined us so that we could finish our tours together.

The Munich raid was uneventful and was immediately followed by a lull in operations. During the next two weeks my logbook shows only three short daylight bombing exercises and a couple of ferry trips to other stations in the Group. When operations resumed against Mannheim on 23rd September we did not appear on the Battle Order. This turned out to have been a good trip to miss as three of the twenty squadron aircraft despatched did not return. But when we were not called up for the next two operations I began to wonder what was wrong. I was just about to knock on the flight commander's door and ask for a reason when I was told to report to the new squadron commander, Wing Commander Fisher. "I see you have been on the squadron longer than anyone, Paddy," said Fisher. "You arrived in early February. What happened?" "Well, Sir, my eardrum was damaged when I was running up my engines before taking off for Wuppertal on 29th May and I didn't fly on operations again until early July." "I have got some good news for you, Paddy." said the Wing Commander. "You've been here long enough. They are running short of instructors at Group and I have been asked to release a crew for instructional duties immediately. I've put your name forward. Go and tell your crew to collect their clearance chits. Your postings should come through in a day or two and then you can go on leave. Well done. Thank you for doing such a good job."

To say I was stunned was putting it mildly. It was over - and we had survived. The rest of the crew didn't believe me at first. Not until I showed them my clearance chit, on which I had already started to collect signatures. First of all we had to thank our ground crew so we took them out to the 'Red Lion' for a few drinks - and then a few more. Our ground crew really had been magnificent. They had worked in all weathers to keep ED944 ready for us to fly and they had seldom failed. Certainly this Queen of all the Lancasters had never let us down and now had brought us safely to the end of our tour. Only now did we realise the strain put on our ground crew when we were flying over Germany. I recalled the occasion when we returned to dispersal after a raid and were met by one of the fitters sheepishly carrying a chest-type parachute. I used a seat-type pack but had anything happened to us the other six crew members would have had only five packs between them. I remembered saying, "I don't want to know whose pack that is but just think about it and make sure you don't forget it again." Not that any such warning was needed after they realised what might have happened. 'Chiefy' Booth was with us and said to me after the others had left, "Your ground crew were inconsolable all through that night. If you hadn't got back I don't know how they would have got over it."

One of the most pleasant 'clearance' stops was, in fact, in the parachute section. We wanted to thank the girls who maintained the parachutes and issued them to the aircrew before each operation. Most aircrew had their lucky parachute girl and always sought her out when collecting his 'chute. We burst into the section and I shouted out, "We're finished, girls. Just called in for a signature and to say thank-you and goodbye." I looked around for the little WAAF who usually gave me my parachute and always wished me luck. I couldn't see her at first but then I noticed her in the back office. She looked distressed and tears were running down her cheeks. Two of the other girls were saying "Go on. Go on." She rushed out of the office, round the other side of the counter, threw her arms around my neck, kissed me and said , "I'm so, so glad."

I had already obtained the squadron commander's signature confirming my operational record and I was just completing my clearance procedure on 5th October when I was again summoned to Wing Commander Fisher's office. "I'm terribly sorry, Paddy. Group won't accept that your crew be short-toured. You are four trips short and they say that's too many. I said I had already told you to clear the station, but they wouldn't change their minds. It is a terrible thing to do to anybody and I'm truly sorry." I felt too choked to say anything so I just stood there - silent. The Squadron Commander went on, "You had better make a start on those four trips so you're on tonight's Battle Order. I wish you and your crew all the luck in the world. I'm sure you'll finish your tour."

I thought the boys took the news rather well. Joe said, "I never really believed it anyway." When I collected my parachute that afternoon my little WAAF burst into tears all over again. The general opinion on the squadron was that it was a rather dirty trick and that Group should have backed up the squadron commander. However, we went to Frankfurt that night and on the following night to Stuttgart. Fighter activity was intense but we returned from both targets without incident. Now we had only to fly over Germany twice more.

Hannover - The Agony and the Ecstasy

'The plane ahead was on fire. Its propellor blades slowed as they feathered, but the flames were getting brighter by the second. The night-fighter would come in again as sure as God made little apples ..... Please God make him go down. He doesn't have to crash, if he'll just go down. Please God, just a thousand feet ... Five hundred, then ... The light from the burning Lancaster was worse. They'll never save it now ... ...the whole sky is ablaze with this bloody dying Lancaster almost touching our wingtip. Make it go down. Shoot it down ... Nothing should hold on like that, it's obscene.'

The above extract from Len Deighton's novel 'Bomber' describes much more vividly than any words of mine could possibly do, my feelings over Hannover on our penultimate operation on the 8th October, 1943. We were flying in 'E' - Easy as our own aircraft was undergoing a major service. The trip had been uneventful until we started our approach to the target, flying straight and level to give our bomb-aimer the best possible chance of hitting the target markers. I had noticed a fighter attack on our port beam which had left a bomber in flames. This aircraft continued its approach towards the target, at the same altitude as ourselves and coming closer to us by the second. We were already committed to our bombing run so all I could do was to wait for either another attack on the. burning aircraft or for its bomb-load to explode as the flames took hold. As the aircraft came nearer I saw it was a Lancaster and I was able to make out the squadron letters - VN - which I knew belonged to 50 Squadron. The tension became unbearable as we both approached the bomb-release point. Fortunately for us, and possibly because the crew had already abandoned ship, the other aircraft dipped a wing and disappeared from sight. Much relieved, we dropped our bombs and returned home safely.

As far as I was concerned, although we ourselves were not attacked, this was probably the worst experience of my entire tour of operations. Had the burning aircraft exploded we could not possibly have survived. In addition, I felt that the flames were bound to attract an enemy pilot who, seeing that the aircraft was already doomed, would turn his attention to the nearest alternative target. Thankfully, neither of these things happened.

Many years after the war, I asked Eric Day, a well-known aviation artist, to paint me a picture of this particular incident. This he did, and his picture is reproduced on the front cover. When the Bomber Command Association was seeking information about the artist, I sent a photograph of Day's painting, together with the following letter:

'Eric Day flew with a good friend of mine, 'Ted' Harker. I believe he was Ted's bomb-aimer. They were involved in one of the last Lancaster raids of the war - on Hitler's 'Eagle's Nest' at Berchtesgaden. Day's painting of this raid hung for many years in the Staff College at Bracknell. When Ted Harker died a few years ago his brother-in-law, Sqn Ldr John Niven DFC, went to the College in the hope of obtaining permission to have a copy made for Ted's widow. Sadly the painting had disappeared and could not be traced.

I met Eric Day when I was on the staff at Bracknell. I remember saying to·him how much I liked his painting and he offered to do one for me if I had any wartime experience I would like recorded. At that time the incident that stood out most vividly (as it still does today) was every bomber pilot's nightmare of two aircraft at the same altitude converging on the same aiming point - and the other poor fellow on fire. This happened on my penultimate operation to Hannover on 8th October, 1943, so I had seen most things by then -

and been shot up a few times - but this situation was something else'.

The Editor of the Newsletter added after the letter: 'The painting clearly shows the 57 Squadron Lancaster DX-E closing in on the blazing Lancaster coded VN-? These letters VN were of course used by 50 Squadron, and Bill Chorley's 'Bomber Command Losses 1943' tells us that 50 Squadron lost DV324, VN-N, on that Hannover raid. Five of the crew (including the pilot) became prisoners-of-war, the other two sadly perished. Bill Chorley writes of Lancaster VN-N: Hit by flak at 21,000feet and crashed at Wilkenburg, 7km SSE from the centre of Hannover'.

My letter, and the Editor's comments, brought a response from an ex-pilot claiming that his was the aircraft shot down. The next issue of the Newsletter carried the following:

'It is not surprising that Eric Day's picture ...... caught the interest of F/L J.C.P. Taylor as he was the pilot of the Lancaster VN-N (DV324) depicted on fire. F/L Taylor, the man-in-the-hot-seat, tells us that Bill Chorley is basically correct except that they were actually hit by a night-fighter (an ME110, he believes) using upward firing cannon during the moment of them releasing their bombs and the flashlight going out. They were hit in the port wing tank which caused a substantial fire. It refused to respond to diving and they were forced to bale out'.

My letter to the Bomber Command Association setting out my recollections of the incident over Hannover on 8th October, 1943, together with the responses that followed, show how easy it is to be mistaken in the heat of battle. In 'Bomber Command Losses 1943' the loss of Lancaster VN-N was attributed to flak, yet the pilot who flew the aircraft maintains that they were shot down by a fighter using upward firing cannon. I am convinced that the aircraft in Eric Day's painting - and still vividly in my memory - was attacked by a night-fighter some minutes short of the target. I clearly saw the fighter's tracer, so if there was only a single enemy aircraft involved, it could not have been armed with upward firing cannon, or 'schräge musik', which made no use of tracer during an attack. I also have no doubt that it was the aircraft's starboard engine that was on fire. In the face of the evidence, I am forced to admit that the mistake was mine, and that I misread the squadron letters on the burning aircraft.

The final trip of my operational tour, some ten days later, was also to Hannover. After the tension of the previous sortie, my last operation was a delight. We had no trouble, bombed on time and on target, and returned safely. On the return journey, instead of the usual gradual descent to give increased airspeed, I set about fulfilling a long-time promise to myself that I would find out what altitude it was possible to attain in a Lancaster - in ED944. Starting from the target at 22,000 feet we climbed slowly upwards. As we climbed, I noticed that the streaks of flame coming from the engines got longer and longer and the exhausts gradually changed colour until they glowed red-hot. I knew what my target height was. I wanted to fly higher than the top of Everest, which I remembered was 29,002 feet. Eventually we got there. We had climbed our Everest and we had finished our tour. We were surely on top of the world.

Chapter 13

The Human Factor

Melting Pot

The bomber crews came from all walks of life. They came from every part of the British Isles and from every corner of the Empire and Commonwealth. The contributions from Canada, Australia and New Zealand were immense, when compared to the population of their countries. The Poles had their own squadrons and flew with a burning intensity of purpose. The neutral Irish were well represented, as were the Americans, most of whom preferred to stay with the RAF rather than transfer to their own Air Forces. Here and there were individuals whose motivation was less obvious; men such as Flight Lieutenant Ciano, a 57 Squadron navigator and distant relative of Mussolini, who was never asked to attack Italian targets. All had much in common: they were young, they were fit, and they wanted to fly.

The Singer Twins

When we joined the squadron the Singer twins from New Zealand were old hands with several operational trips behind them. Peter and Tony were both pilots, each with his own crew. They were almost identical; only those who knew them well could tell them apart. Peter had already had one close call. He was flying one of the ninety-six Lancasters that carried out the famous low-level daylight raid on the armaments factory at Le Creusot on 17th October, 1942. On the outward journey his windscreen was shattered by a bird - later identified as a partridge - and his flight engineer temporarily blinded. In spite of the engineer's injuries, and the crew's discomfort, he pressed on and successfully attacked the target. After one particular operation Peter became most agitated and unsettled at de-briefing. 'Tony's in trouble. Something is wrong. I know

The Singer Twins

it." The usual stragglers obtained their permission to land but there was still no sign of Tony. Then, quite suddenly, Peter's mood changed. He smiled and said "He's OK." Ten minutes later there was the unmistakable sound of a Lancaster over the airfield and very soon Tony and his crew were telling their story. They had had a brush with a fighter, lost an engine and it had been a long trip home. The odds against the twins both completing their tours must have been considerable but they survived. Sadly they were unable to enjoy their good luck for long. Peter met his death in a car accident in 1953 and Tony died shortly after.

Joe

Without a doubt, Joe was the most handsome airman on the squadron. He flew as mid-upper gunner with one of the 'A' Flight crews. He was tall, slim and broad shouldered and his striking, almost perfect, features were topped by a mass of wavy brown hair. When he walked into the pubs and dance halls of Lincoln in his immaculate sergeant's uniform every female eye turned in his direction. As well as being attractive to the ladies, Joe was also a first-rate air gunner. He spent hours in his turret, polishing his ammunition to prevent stoppages and ensuring that his guns worked efficiently. To this end, he sought out the armourers; they all knew Joe and were only too willing to help. Sadly, on the night he died, Joe did not fire a single round. It is doubtful if he even saw the fighter that sent a cannon shell into his turret, killing him instantly. The aircraft returned safely to base and the medics in due course removed Joe's body. The job of cleaning up Joe's turret was the responsibility of the armourers and more than fifty years later I sat next to one of these armourers, Roy Jones, at a squadron reunion. I asked if he had known Joe. "Everyone knew Joe," he said. "The worst job I ever had to do was clean out his turret the morning after he was killed." My thoughts went back over the years to those striking features. "Was it true ..." I started to say. He cut me short. "Yes it was." Roy's voice was full of emotion. "Maybe he was too handsome but that was a terrible way to go."

Ted

Ted Stanton was an instructor at the Air Gunners' School at RAF Stormy Down. Teaching gunners the theory of defence against fighter attack - how different it could all turn out in practice. Most of the instructors had completed a tour of operations but Ted had never seen a shot fired in anger. He was most unhappy about this and after some of his colleagues had made unkind remarks in the Mess, Ted had applied to join an operational squadron. But Ted was a very good instructor and as very good instructors were hard to find his application was turned down. Nothing daunted, he asked for a personal interview with the Station Commander. If Ted couldn't do a tour of operations could he perhaps fly on just one trip so that he could at least know what it was like over there and tell his pupils accordingly. The Station Commander agreed to Ted's request and rang up his old friend who was commanding 57

Squadron. Ted was duly attached to Scampton where he struck up a rapport with our two gunners. That is why our crew had one extra member for the raid on Essen on 27th May.

There was only one place I could find room for Ted and that was in the front turret. Of course, if he wanted to see what it was really like over Essen there was no better place to be. Essen had deservedly earned the reputation among aircrews as the toughest target. I had been twice before so I knew what to expect, or at least I thought I did until I saw what was in front of us as we approached the town. The flak barrage was intense and seemed to cover all the altitudes being flown by the various types of bombers. Searchlights probed the sky in all directions; at least two aircraft were coned and were vainly trying to escape. I saw three bombers on fire and watched as two more crews met their Maker in hideous eruptions of high octane and high explosives. Down below the fires were burning fiercely around the red and green markers of the Pathfinders and the exploding photo-flashes enabled the bombers to record the accuracy of their individual attacks. I was convinced that it was impossible for any aircraft to fly into this maelstrom and survive. But survive we did.

I had not given too much thought to Ted during the flight although I had to ask him to keep his turret still during our bombing run. Once we had crossed the coast I told him to leave his turret and stand behind me. I think he was happy to stretch his legs. He had not spoken since leaving the target until we were in the crew bus. He said, "Do you chaps have to go through that every night?" Joe our wireless operator, was quick to answer, "No, mate. Only fifteen more bloody nights and that's it." Ted went back to Stormy Down the next day, a better instructor to be sure, for he had been to war.

Trevor

I will call him Trevor although I have no idea what his first name was. I do remember his surname but this is something I will never disclose. Trevor appeared one day in the flight commander's office. He was a flight lieutenant and wore the ribbon of the Distinguished Flying Cross. He had difficulty in walking and leant heavily on a stick. Trevor sported a heavy moustache and his face had a peculiar texture, almost as if he had been badly burned, yet all his features were untouched. Those who saw him wondered what had happened to him and why he spent day after day in the flight commander's office. I got to know a little more about Trevor when I was summoned to the squadron commander's office and told that I would be taking Trevor that night as second pilot. He exchanged the usual platitudes with the crew before take-off but once airborne he remained silent. I pointed out in turn the searchlight belt on the Dutch coast, the various flak hot-spots and the inevitable aircraft either coned or falling in flames to the earth below. Trevor merely nodded as each incident unfolded. As we approached the target, however, his manner changed. He buried his head in his hands and I could hear a low moaning through the intercom. I tapped him on the shoulder but he pushed my hand away. Eventually the moaning became so bad that I motioned to Stan to pull out his jack-plug. Trevor did not raise his head until we were well clear of the target and he did not speak again. As we taxied to dispersal after landing I saw Freddie's car in close attendance. Trevor left the aircraft without a word. He was met at the bottom of the ladder by Freddie who caught his arm and led him to the waiting car. I never saw Trevor again. Early next morning I was told to report to the Squadron Commander at once. He asked me about Trevor's reaction to the previous night's operation. When I had told him he said, "I want you to forget about last night. On no account are you to put the flight lieutenant's name in your log book. Understood?" "Certainly, Sir," I said. Freddie went on, "Last year he was flying Wellingtons in North Africa and was shot down into the Med. He drifted in a dinghy for more than a week with a broken leg and without water. He watched his crew die one by one and when picked up he couldn't speak and was barely alive. A return to ops was his wish but he wasn't sure if he could cope.

Obviously he could not. There are those who would hold last night's trip against him but I want to make sure they never have the chance. That's why, as far as everyone else is concerned, he didn't fly with you last night."

The Americans

The first Americans arrived on the squadron in early summer. Jack Russell and his navigator, Dick Wright, stood out in their olive-green jackets and 'pink pants'. They fitted in well; we didn't ask how much they were paid and they didn't tell us. Jack Russell was dark-haired, thick-set, and spoke with a mid-western drawl. Dick was tall and slim with a mop of fair hair. Both men were quickly accepted by the rest of the squadron. Jack Russell and his corn-cob pipe were inseparable. Although he denied ever smoking in his aircraft, we found out by chance that this was untrue. After the debacle at Pilsen when the entire force dropped their bombs on a lunatic asylum instead of the Skoda Works, the Commander-in-Chief ordered all squadrons back to the practice ranges. Every day for a week we dropped our practice bombs on the Wainfleet range on the Fens and for good measure we carried out three night attacks on the small island of St. Tudwals, a bird sanctuary lying a few miles off the Welsh coast to the north of Cardigan Bay. On one of our 'attacks', which were carried out under operational conditions, keeping radio silence and showing no lights, we noticed another Lancaster at the same altitude a short distance to starboard. I watched the other aircraft intently, ready to take evasive action if necessary, and was intrigued to see an orange glow appear in the cockpit at frequent intervals. In the light of an exploding photo-flash, Stan was able to make out the aircraft markings and shouted out, "It's the Yanks." We quickly deduced that the glow was coming from Jack Russell's corn-cob. Jack admitted afterwards that he had been caught in the act but assured us that he never, never smoked on operations. Another American pilot joined the squadron at Scampton as a Royal Air Force officer. By the time we moved to East Kirkby he was wearing

American uniform. Don West was small, dapper, prematurely bald and the ultimate in American charm. For some weeks he and I dated two lovely sisters in Boston and for this reason only I was sorry to be posted away at the end of my tour. It was not until I read Anne Doward's splendid tribute to her father[1] some fifty years later that I learned that Don had lost his life less than two weeks after I had left the squadron. He was shot down by a fighter on the way to Dusseldorf and only his bomb-aimer and navigator survived. His name is on the wall of the Chapel of Remembrance at East Kirkby among those of more than a thousand airmen who took off from the airfield and did not return.

Fear and Faith

Though I fly through the valley of the shadow of death I will fear no evil, for thou art with me, thy rod and thy staff they comfort me.

23rd Psalm (Adapted)

I have heard many aircrew members boast that they were never afraid throughout their operational tour. In every case, however, that tour had been completed and those who spoke were sheltering in the quiet backwater of a training unit. I cannot remember any man making such a claim on my operational squadron where the prospect of danger and possibly death might only be a few hours away. At the time I was convinced that every member of every bomber crew experienced fear in some degree. It was, after all, no more than the body's natural reaction to danger or the threat of danger. If controlled, it could act as a powerful stimulant to an individual's mental and physical response. If not, it could lead

1   'No Verse Can Say' - the story of Anne Doward's search for the facts behind the death of her father - Pilot Officer Ernest Tansley of 57 Squadron.

to panic, when all would be lost. Although the presence of the other members of the crew was a tremendous help, the battle to control one's fear was entirely a personal one. Most found it difficult to turn to others for help; each man tackled the problem in his own way. Happily the great majority succeeded in keeping their fear under control, thus enabling them to carry out their responsibilities as indispensable members of their crews. Shortly after the war someone asked me how I had felt flying over Germany. I replied that I was apprehensive all the time, afraid most of the time, and terrified more than once. On reflection, that was an accurate statement and I would not wish to change it all these years later.

My personal battle against fear was made so much easier by my faith. I had faith in my aircraft; the Lancaster was supreme - I knew there was none better. I had faith in my own ability to fly the aircraft and in the competence of my friends who flew with me. I had faith in the ground crews who always kept the aircraft we flew in superb condition. I had faith in my squadron commander, who never asked anyone to do what he was not willing to do himself. I had faith in the Commander-in-Chief, whose inspired leadership was acknowledged on every squadron. If my faith was shaken sometimes by mistakes made by the planning staff who carried out his orders, I always believed that their intentions were good and that the survival of the crews was paramount in their planning, as it was in his.

Above all, I had faith in my God. I turned to him during every operation, sometimes it was just a simple prayer before take-off, sometimes - when the target area looked truly awesome - I went through my version of the 23rd Psalm as we were running in towards the aiming point. On one occasion these words were broadcast to the crew as I had left my microphone on. Halfway through I realised what was happening and switched off. Immediately a voice said, "For God's sake keep it going, Skip. It makes me feel so much better." To this day I do not know who had spoken. On the occasions when the danger was most acute, I always prayed specifically for our deliverance. Each time my prayer was answered.

Several times during our tour of operations we found ourselves in a situation where it looked unlikely that we would survive. Somehow, with a little skill and a lot of luck, we came through. In addition, there must have been countless occasions unknown to us when we were close to disaster: a collision narrowly averted, a near miss from flak, a German night fighter passing us by. I find it hard to believe that we completed our tour when so many others did not. It was neither skill nor experience that brought us through, for fate was cruelly indifferent to both. It might have been luck, but we had no right to expect that the dice would roll so often in our favour. I remain convinced that I was kept alive, and with me my crew, by my faith in God, who afforded me His constant protection. Of course, others in the crew might well have sought help from above. Joe, our wireless operator, now tells me that, before every trip, he prayed for our safe return. Some of the others may also have said a prayer for our safety. I just do not know, for this was a personal matter like the fight against fear. For my own part, I never doubted that my God would bring me safely through. I still have doubts about His purpose but that is another story.

Chapter 14

Aftermath

Order of Battle

On the morning of 30th July, 1943, Joe Coxall, our wireless operator, took down from the Sergeants' Mess notice board the Battle Order for the previous night's operation. "Someday, someone, might be interested in this," he thought, as he tucked it into his inside tunic pocket. Almost sixty years later he found the Battle Order at the back of one of his cupboards and posted it to me. The Order authorised 57 Squadron to carry out an attack on Hamburg, the third of the four great raids on that city. This was the raid on which nine of the squadron's aircraft were, due to a briefing error, given the wrong time-on-target and arrived over Hamburg after all the other attackers had left for home. The aircraft flown by Flight Sergeants Allwright and Parker were shot down. The names of the fourteen men making up the crews of these two aircraft stand out as a rebuke to someone's incompetence.

What memories are stirred by the other names on this single sheet of paper. Tony Gobbie, the practical joker with the dark jowls, flying in 'E'-Easy with Sergeant Lamble as his rear gunner. Five weeks later Lamble would be in our rear turret over Berlin and would play a major part in repelling a determined night-fighter attack. Gobbie's aircraft was shot down after we left the squadron but happily both he and Lamble survived and spent the rest of the war as prisoners. 'Slab' Irwin, the Australian sheep farmer in 'W'-Willie; he and I were rather similar in appearance, so much so that he always called me 'Brother'. The previous 'W'-Willie, being flown by 'Dutchy' Haye, had been shot down crossing the coast on the way to Pilsen on 13th May. 'Dutchy' had always claimed that if he came down in his native Holland he would be back with the squadron in a week. He made good his boast.

Flying as second pilot to Squadron Leader Crocker in 'BAR O' was the new squadron commander, Wing Commander Haskill. Sadly, Haskill and his crew would lose their lives on the Peenemünde raid three weeks later. Malcolm Crocker, an American, was 'B' Flight Commander; shortly after we finished our tour, 'B' Flight became the nucleus of the newly-constituted 630 Squadron. Crocker was promoted wing commander and took command. On returning from his refresher course with a commission, 'Burma' Gibson, our old navigator, joined Crocker's crew and completed his tour. I do not know what happened to him afterwards. My abiding memory will always be the dark face looking over my shoulder towards the target when he should have been working out the course for our return journey.

Hidden Treasure

During my time on 57 Squadron, my aunt's sister was a civil servant in the Personnel Branch of the Air Ministry. When I met her shortly after the war she told me that she knew about my DFC some considerable time before the award was gazetted. She did not tell me, however, that she had taken a photocopy of the final draft of my citation. More than fifty years after the event - and long after her death - this photocopy was found among her effects and eventually came into my possession.

In view of the high degree of secrecy to which such matters were subject, this document, although maybe not unique, is extremely rare. The officer who drafted the citation initially, probably the Intelligence Officer on 57 Squadron, failed to reconcile the date with the target attacked, a mistake that was picked up by the Awards Officer in the Air Ministry. His manuscript amendments were incorporated in the final entry in the 'London Gazette'.

Battle Order for the Night of 29th July, 1943

No. 57 Squadron, R.A.F. - NIGHT FLYING PROGRAMME - 29th July, 1943.

A/C.	CAPT.	NAV.	F/ENG.	W/OPRT.	B/AIMER.	M/UPPER.	R/GUNNER.
U.	F/L.GREIG.	P/O.ADAMS.	P/O.NASH.	P/O.HARRIS.	P/O.RANDOLPH.	SGT.MURRAY.	F/S.ROBERTS.
E.	P/O.GOBBIE.	F/O.GARDNER.	SGT.HEMMINGS.	F/L.SCOTT.	SGT.JACKSON.	SGT.SHERBOURNE.	SGT.LAMBLE.
I.	P/O.MCCREA.	SGT.GLENCROSS.	SGT.GUY.	SGT.OXALL.	SGT.ADAMS.	SGT.ALLEN.	SGT.SHERRETT.
X.	P/O.WEST.	P/O.BUGGEY.	SGT.BELL.	SGT.MCKERWIN.	F/L.EILLOT.	SGT.HEATON.	P/L.SHERBUNDS.
C.	F/S.ALLWRIGHT.	SGT.EIGEN.	F/L.KENNEDY.	SGT.BELL.	SGT.OMEAUD.	SGT.SLADE.	SGT.BRACKEN.
A.	SGT.BROWNING.	SGT.HALLETT.	SGT.SMITH.	SGT.MADDOCKS.	F/L.HILL.	SGT.MARLOW.	SGT.BRAGG.
H.	F/O.EGGINS.	F/O.CROWTHER.	SGT.MAPLEDRAM.	SGT.PATTERSON.	SGT.SMITH(760)	SGT.PURSBY.	SGT.BUNKER.
Z.	SGT.PARKER.	SGT.PORTEOUS.	SGT.CRUMBLEY.	SGT.O'LEARY.	SGT.MARSDON.	SGT.READ.	SGT.WHARTON.
O.	S/L.CROCKER.	P/O.JONES.	SGT.STRINGER.	SGT.NYE.	SGT.HARKNESS?	SGT.LAMB.	SGT.JOIN.
	W/C.HASKELL						
O.	F/L.WILSON.	SGT.BURNS.	SGT.PETTEFAR.	SGT.FLOYD.	SGT.GARMENT.	SGT.MAJOR.	SGT.BROADBENT.
J.	F/O.LEVY.	SGT.MCKILLOP.	SGT.LYNN.	SGT.THOMAS.	SGT.MAY.	SGT.PERRY.	SGT.CROWTHER.
H.	P/O.PRATT.	SGT.SMART.	SGT.HILTON.	SGT.CRAWLEY.	SGT.BLOIS.	SGT.BROCKS.	SGT.WILLIAMS.
K.	F/S.GIFFORD.	SGT.AGNEW.	SGT.LUKE.	SGT.TANNER.	SGT.HARRISON.	SGT.CAMPBELL.	SGT.MORRIS.
M.	SGT.MOORES.	SGT.TROMPSON.	SGT.TOMPKIN.	SGT.MCRCLIFFE.	SGT.CUSHING.	SGT.GOLDING.	F/S.HUGHES.
V.	SGT.RYRIE.	SGT.LEDINGHAM.	SGT.JOHNSON.	SGT.SHERRIFF.	F/O.POW.	SGT.HAWKING.	F/S.CONWAY.
T.	F/S.PARKER.	SGT.SMYTHE.	SGT.LANCASTER.	SGT.WALTERS.	P/O.MATTHEWS.	SGT.CARPENTER.	SGT.MADDOCKS.
Y.	F/O.WHITTAM.	F/O.BROWN.	SGT.SIMONS.	P/O.BELCHER.	F/O.MCGONAGLE.	SGT.WALLACE.	SGT.MARDEN.
W.	F/S.IRWIN.	SGT.KNOWLES.	SGT.GRIFFITH.	SGT.SANDERSON.	F/O.MCROBBIE.	SGT.DAWKINS.	SGT.REAP.
K.	SGT.HARGREAVE.P/O.DUNHLEY.	SGT.REEVE.	SGT.HUXTABLE.SGT.WHITTLE.	SGT.HALL.			SGT.SMITH(775)

DUTY NAV.	DUTY F/ENG.	DUTY W/OPRT.	DUTY A/GNR.	DUTY B/AIMER.
W/C.BROWN.	SGT.THOMAS.	SGT.BLANC.	SGT.MCFALLS.	P/O.JOHNSON.

Draft of Citation for DFC

Pilot Officer William Ernest McCREA (146428), Royal Air Force Volunteer Reserve, No. 57 Squadron.   This officer has completed many successful operations, including such targets as Berlin, Hamburg and many industrial centres in the Ruhr. He has displayed great skill and leadership and his efforts throughout have been featured by determination of a high standard. One night in September, 1943, when returning from an attack on Hanover, his aircraft was intercepted by a fighter. A prolonged combat ensued but coolly and skilfully, Pilot Officer McCrea finally succeeded in out-manoeuvring his adversary. The bomber sustained much damage but this pilot flew it safely to base. He displayed great courage and resolution in trying circumstances.

EXTRACT FROM   AIR MINISTRY RECORDS

In Retrospect

In looking back after an interval of sixty years I have had no difficulty in recalling the incidents that took place during my operational tour. These memories will remain clear for the rest of my life . The words I have used in the communications between crew members may not have been those actually spoken on the nights in question but the substance has not been changed.

Losses during my time on 57 Squadron were severe and the situation deteriorated further over the ensuing months. Bomber Command themselves were, in my opinion, partly to blame. Pilots were not kept fully informed of current operational tactics. They had been taught to handle their aircraft competently but apart from a single trip as second pilot they were largely left to their own devices over enemy territory. I spent the last eighteen months of the war as a flying instructor at an Operational Training Unit. During my tour of operations I had been hit by flak, coned by searchlights and attacked by night fighters. I had flown a damaged bomber back to base, lost my way over enemy territory and found myself 'fogged out' on my return. Yet I was never asked to pass on this experience to trainee pilots who, with their crews, were shortly to join operational squadrons. The fact that new bomber crews did not know what to expect often proved too great a handicap and many perished before gaining the experience that would have helped to ensure their survival.

Bombers Command's greatest mistake was the failure to counter the introduction by the Luftwaffe of its most effective weapon: 'schräge musik' ('slanting music'). The addition of two upward-firing cannon to the ME110's conventional armament allowed the German pilots to approach unseen and attack the vulnerable underbellies of the British bombers. No tracer was used, making the attacking aircraft and its method virtually invisible to the rest of the bomber force. It is claimed that Bomber Command did not know of the existence of this deadly weapon until hostilities had ceased. This lack of knowledge must have been one of the costliest intelligence failures of the whole war. The extent of the threat, and the severity of the attrition, can be encapsulated in a period of nineteen minutes on 21st February, 1945, during which time Major Heinz Schnaufer shot down seven four-engined bombers in his Messerschmitt 110 fitted with 'schräge musik'[1]

Bomber Command did have the means of giving their crews some measure of protection from 'schräge musik'. This was by ensuring that pilots changed the position of their aircraft continuously when over enemy territory. For my own part, I used the corkscrew, perhaps a milder version than the one I used when attacked, but the movement was continuous nevertheless. Others used a banking search or compensating changes in course. On the other hand, many pilots flew straight and level for long periods. Some ignored movement completely. One of these was Etienne 'Lofty' Maze, who laid his mattress alongside mine on the floor of a luxury apartment in Abbey Road in August, 1941, when we both donned RAF uniform for the first time. 'Lofty' Maze graduated to Halifaxes and his trips to and from his targets were normally completed on auto-pilot[2]. At the end of his tour he was appointed ADC to the Commander-in-Chief. It is possible that his disdain for the need to keep changing position had some influence on Bomber Command policy. I remain convinced that my version of the corkscrew kept us free from fighter attack. The only time we sustained significant damage from a night-fighter was when I had to abandon the manoeuvre in order to maintain height in a sub-standard aircraft.

The first recorded use of 'schräge musik' by the Luftwaffe was during the raid against the Rocket Research Establishment at

1   From 'Out of the Blue' by Laddie Lucas

2   From 'Bomber Command' by Max Hastings

Peenemünde on 17th August, 1943. It is interesting to note the comments of one of the German pilots, Unteroffizier Walter Holker:

"We climbed up again and found another one immediately - a Lancaster this time. I think this one had seen us because he started his weaving, evasive manoeuvre. It was difficult to get under this bomber when he was flying this way ...."[3]

At the RAF Staff College after the war, I talked with German night-fighter pilots who confirmed that they had seldom attacked bombers that were seen to be taking evasive action. They also agreed that only the very best of their pilots were able to stay with a bomber during the evasive manoeuvre and conceded that the great majority had difficulty in making a kill unless the bomber was flying straight and level. These views were consistent with those of the greatest German night-fighter ace of all, Major Heinz Schnaufer, who was credited with the destruction of 121 night bombers and whose exploits have already been mentioned above. The following extracts are taken from the transcript of his interrogation in May 1945[4]:

'When approaching from astern and below for an attack with forward firing guns ('schräge musik'), if the bomber corkscrewed, it was most difficult for the fighter to gather speed quickly enough to follow it down in the initial dive.'

3   From 'The Peenemünde Raid' by Martin Middlebrook

4   From 'Fighting the Bombers - The Luftwaffe's struggle against the Allied Bomber Offensive. D.C. Isby (Ed.)

'On the approach, if the bomber commenced corkscrewing .... the fighter pilots would usually break away .....'

Schnaufer also had something to say about the undoubted star of the bomber war: Butch Harris's 'shining sword' - the Lancaster:

' ... the general manoeuvrability of the Lancaster, and the most violent manoeuvres carried out by some Lancasters he had attacked, amazed him.'

Reflections

Over past years, I have had many hallucinations and nightmares due to my experiences but, thankfully, I have been able to dismiss them immediately as part of my sub-conscious and they have had no impact on my life. If these hallucinations were designed to make me feel remorse for my actions they have not succeeded. Of course, I was horrified when I read the reports and, many years later, watched the German newsreels showing the effects of the Hamburg firestorm. No person who calls himself a human being could look at such scenes and fail to feel the utmost compassion. At the same time, I have never experienced any feeling of guilt. They 'sowed the wind' and did indeed 'reap the whirlwind'. Without reservation, I am proud to have been part of the bomber force. For those who, after the war, sought to besmirch the character of the bomber crews and their Commander, I have nothing but contempt. If they could have taken Ted Stanton's place in the front turret on his trip to Essen they might well have been less critical.

Epilogue

All of this took place a long time ago and those of us who are left are now old men. Chris, who has helped so much in the writing of this book, has a cliff-top home in Devon and enjoys his magnificent views out to sea. Sadly, he is not in good health and knows that he is fighting his last battle. In his own words, the 'Grim Reaper', who had passed him by so often, is finally closing in. 'Joe' Coxall, our wireless operator, married his Edna, who spent many long nights anxiously waiting for his safe return. They now live in a house called 'Scampton'. When we met up again he told me that Taffy had died some five years earlier. I have the fondest memories of our Welshman: he was an excellent bomb-aimer, best man at my wedding, and the life and soul of every party. I saw in Martin Middlebrook's book on 'The Battle of Hamburg' that Stan Guy, our flight engineer, had been a contributor. I believe that after the war he went to either South Africa or Rhodesia, as it was then, but I have not heard from him. John Kimber, who was our rear gunner for six of our last eight trips, lives near to me in the southern suburbs of London. He, like Chris, went on to complete a second tour and both were awarded well-deserved DFCs. Not too many air gunners survived fifty operations . 'Ace' Clarke took his wounds back to Canada, but a recent attempt to trace him through the Saskatchewan authorities has been unsuccessful. As for the others who flew with me, I do not know how they fared. I remember them all and thank them for helping us beat the odds in the night skies over Germany.

Bibliography

'Bomber Harris - His Life and Times' by Henry Probert

'Bomber Command' by Max Hastings

'The Battle of Hamburg' by Martin Middlebrook

'The Peenemünde Raid' by Martin Middlebrook

'Out of the Blue' by Laddie Lucas

'No Verse Can Say' by Anne Doward

Fighting the Bombers - The Luftwaffe's struggle against the Allied Bomber Offensive. D.C. Isby (Editor)

Memorial to the aircrew of Nos. 57 and 630
Squadrons who took-off from RAF East Kirkby
and did not return.